ALIZÉE FROMENT

The Horses

WHO MADE ME

A Journey to a Horsemanship Philosophy

TRAFALGAR SQUARE
North Pomfret, Vermont

First published in 2024 by
Trafalgar Square Books
North Pomfret, Vermont 05053

Disclaimer of Liability
The author and publisher shall have neither liability nor responsibility to any person or entity with respect to any loss or damage caused or alleged to be caused directly or indirectly by the information contained in this book. While the book is as accurate as the author can make it, there may be errors, omissions, and inaccuracies.

Trafalgar Square Books encourages the use of approved safety helmets in all equestrian sports and activities.

Trafalgar Square Books certifies that the content in this book was generated by a human expert on the subject, and the content was edited, fact-checked, and proofread by human publishing specialists with a lifetime of equestrian knowledge. TSB does not publish books generated by artificial intelligence (AI).

Library of Congress Cataloging-in-Publication Data
Names: Froment, Alizée, 1987- author.
Title: The horses who made me : a journey to a horsemanship philosophy /
  Alizée Froment.
Description: North Pomfret, Vermont : Trafalgar Square Books, 2023. |
  Includes index.
Identifiers: LCCN 2023014889 (print) | LCCN 2023014890 (ebook) | ISBN
  9781646012152 (paperback) | ISBN 9781646011469 (epub)
Subjects: LCSH: Dressage riders--France--Biography. | Horsemen and
  horsewomen--France--Biography. | Horsemanship--France--Anecdotes. |
  Horses--Anecdotes--Biography. | Human-animal relationships--Anecdotes.
Classification: LCC SF309.482.F76 A3 2023 (print) | LCC SF309.482.F76
  (ebook) | DDC 798.2/3092 [B]--dc23/eng/20230411
LC record available at https://lccn.loc.gov/2023014889
LC ebook record available at https://lccn.loc.gov/2023014890

All photographs courtesy of the author's private collection and Morgan Froment Photography except: pp 2, 3, 123, 152, 175, 182, 183 (Lena Matu); pp. 125, 135, 151, 167 *top right*, 180, 181, 190, 191 (Martine De Leeuw/ Bellavie Photography); p. 124 *top left* (Petra Kerschbaum); pp. 106, 136, 141 (Elise Levrault); p. 174 (Helena Massa Photography); pp. 184, 185 (Alain Laurioux); p. 189 (Drieka Joeris)

Book design by *Katarzyna Misiukanis–Celińska (https://misiukanis-artstudio.com)*
Typefaces: *Playfair Display, PT Serif,* and *Sloop*
Cover design by *RM Didier*

Printed in China
10 9 8 7 6 5 4 3 2 1

– TO MY BELOVED –

Alizée Froment

– WITH SULTAN –

EPIGRAPH

THE BOY DIDN'T KNOW
WHAT A PERSON'S PERSONAL LEGEND WAS.

"It's what you have always wanted to accomplish.
Everyone, when they are young, knows what their
Personal Legend is. At that point in their lives,
everything is clear and everything is possible.
They are not afraid to dream, and to yearn for everything
they would like to see happen to them in their lives.
But, as time passes, a mysterious force begins
to convince them that it will be impossible
for them to realize their Personal Legend."

–

PAULO COELHO,
The Alchemist

PROLOGUE

Being with horses and being a rider
means you never stop questioning yourself.
With each horse who becomes
part of your journey, you have to be ready
to start from square one.

With Mistral, my soulmate.

Of

course, each horse will make you grow, learn, improve...but in order for that to happen, you will have to be ready to face different challenges, understand new things, find other solutions, and search for parallel paths.

There are no two identical horses. The key to a trusting and successful relationship with each horse in your life is to adapt yourself. Just like humans, horses have their own personalities, mindsets, moods, and strengths and weaknesses. They will also evolve along the journeys they take with you in different ways. The answer that worked yesterday might not be the one that works today and could be even less so tomorrow. This is where your responsibility starts, because it's how you can help horses grow into the best version of themselves, or be a human of no help—or even bring out their worst.

In this journey, doubt is your worst enemy as well as your best friend. When a mentor can doubt himself openly *without* betraying the trust of those counting on him, it guides him toward always questioning himself and his choices—a step that is mandatory to give his horses the opportunity to truly shine from inside, as well as from outside. And that's what makes all the difference.

In my now more than 30 years of life, from a child in a "pony club" to my days as a professional rider, I've had the chance to meet

many amazing ponies and horses, each of them deeply different. Each of them "made me" into the human and horseman I am today. And the most difficult stories always ended up being the ones that made me grow the most.

Of course, I would fill 10 books if I wrote about every horse I have known, so I had to make difficult choices to determine the stories I would share here and now. In these pages, you will meet Pil-Pil, Bengal, Shapati, Kazan, Betty-Boop, Goliat, Foy, Clyde, Ice, Lambrusco, Donatello, Joeris, the one and only Mistral, Sultan, Pirate, and Hermès. But my heart will never forget Kataclop, Mandarine, Champion, Bella, Gibraltar, Gaufrette, Germanicus, Naxos, Di Magic, Sir Rubinstein, Walkuere, Ehrendorf, Aslan, J'Adore, Ballerine, Rigoletto, and all the others who crossed my path and helped me grow in one way or another.

The biggest difficulty of the equestrian art in each of its forms is that humans don't speak the horse's language. That's where all our problems begin. With this in mind, we need to always remember that being good to a horse means being fair to him, above all. One of the most important things I have learned about being fair is that horses need a leader or a mentor by their side in order to feel safe. That's how they were created. Wild, they would choose the strongest of their herd to trust and follow. Alone, the horse knows instinctively he must become the strong one to protect himself...or die. *Your horse needs you to become his "safety*

place" before you become his best friend. This doesn't mean you have to be tough; it means you have to be trustworthy. Respecting and loving him is giving him this mentorship because that's how he will learn to feel safe, which will lead him to become self-confident and empowered.

But being a good mentor is not that simple. It's all about finding the right balance. You need to listen to your horse in order to understand him. You need to leave him some space in order to let his true personality grow and shine. You need to give him your trust in order to earn his. But, as you would do with your own child, you have to give the horse straight lines to follow, help him understand and acknowledge his reactions to different situations in order to give him the keys to overcome them, and determine boundaries to respect, because that's also what will help him be able to become the best version of himself. It is this that you have to learn every day, because it is clearly the most difficult thing to do. Being fair. Being right. Knowing how and when to say no. Knowing how to react in an appropriate way and how to handle your own emotions, fears, and doubts. We all have to face these challenges when working with horses, and we all make mistakes. Mistakes can happen. What can't happen is to not learn from them.

In these pages, you will find no miracle secret, but you will discover, step by step, how I grew with each of my horses, the perpetual questions I found and still find every single day along my way, and some of the answers my horses have given me. Because the truth is, there are no better teachers than our horses.

Here you will meet the horses and ponies
who first shared with me the scent of
a freedom that would later guide my entire life.
These were golden years, filled with love, games,
discoveries guided by instinct, and friendship.

Pil-Pil • *Bengal* • *Shapati* • *Kazan* • *Betty Boop*

act I

pony time

With Shapati.

AS I began writing these lines, Bengal, a beautiful, homebred, ebony-colored Shetland born in 1988, had just closed his eyes peacefully for the last time, in our family garden, my parents beside him. My daughter Louise and I had just flown to the south of France to spend Halloween with my family. When we flew over the clouds, Louise asked me if she could go with Bengal for a walk bareback as she had enjoyed so much the previous summer. I told her she could as he had always been in good shape, but before we could even go to hug him hello upon our arrival, his body had decided suddenly that it was time to go.

Of all the ponies who were with me my entire life—saw me born and watched me become the woman I am today from their peaceful retirement in the field— Kazan is now the only one who remains, and I know that even if today he is still dashing, he is 41 years old, and having lost one by one his best friends during the past five years, he will most likely follow them soon. He has always been the "chief." He has remained glorious to the end. But how long will he want to stay here, now that his entire herd is gone? One thing is sure, and that is that the day he decides to join his departed friends, he will take a very big part of my family's hearts with him. Each of these golden ponies has been a huge part of us. Some of them were there before me, for decades. They are a part of our history. They are a part of our identity.

To me, these ponies are my dearest memories, the witnesses of all my first steps, discoveries, failures, and successes. They are my entire childhood, and I can tell you that I was the happiest child in the world. Thinking about those times is and will forever be a source of comfort. What these ponies offered me is far from the spotlights, podiums, and standing ovations I have since experienced. What I had with them was not about competitions, shows, or anything with a precise goal. It was all about friendship, games, fun, education, bareback races in wheat fields, and sleep under the stars. They taught me what unvarnished happiness looks like. There is not a single morning that I do not wake up and begin seeking the pure, true, deep sensations and emotions I discovered thanks to my childhood ponies. They showed me how magical the world can be and wrote it with an indelible ink in every single cell of my body.

Writing these pages will make them immortal. I owe them that much. For more than instilling in me a passion and love for horses, they also passed on to me the two keys that would guide and define my entire life thereafter: *magic* and *freedom*. They are me...or I am them. They defined who I am. *They* are the ones who made me.

Mum introducing me to Pil-Pil.

Pil-Pil

The unconditional trust

His name was Pil-Pil. He was the very first one. A black-and-white Shetland pony, almost as wide as he was tall, with a face like a Thelwell cartoon. Of course, my memories of him are vague as I was literally climbing on him in our yard when I was two years old. But Pil-Pil gave me a blind confidence with horses.

We lived in Paris with my mother at the time, but during each holiday, we headed south, where the family farmhouse that was my grandparents' was located, and where my mother organized, for nearly 30 wonderful years, summer camps to teach children how to ride.

While my mother was working in her office, I would bring a bucket close to Pil-Pil—who, as the mascot of the place, roamed freely—turn it face down,

With Pil-Pil, my first horse friend,
through my earliest years.

jump on it, cling to his mane, and climb until I was happily in place on his back with a big smile on my face. Not once did he run away or even seem to say, *Hey, not now, little girl!* Pil-Pil took care of me with patience and stolidity. He was my babysitter, and my first best friend.

When I was three, Pil-Pil and I started to follow the "big rides" in the countryside with the children attending my mum's camp. Pil-Pil and I were always at the end of the line, followed by Mum on her trusty Sherpa. Apparently, it was not uncommon for me to end up falling asleep and even snoring to the rhythm of Pil-Pil's footsteps as he followed his friends in front. I trusted him fully, entirely. Being on his back was as natural and safe to me as being in my house. I have no idea how old he was at that time. I just know that he died at home, in his late thirties, peacefully, and surrounded by all my family. He was my first horse friend.

Then came others, of course, as I started riding once a week at a barn (what we call a "pony club") near Paris when I was six years old. But I will leave Mandarine, Kataclop, Coco, Champion, Petit Sauvage, and the others cantering in my memories, very close to my heart. That's where they will continue to live, until my last breath. They each were a stepping stone in my journey, and each one of them has been important.

Bengal

Bengal

The one who taught me to never give up

Born a few months after I came into the world, Bengal was a homebred cross between a Shetland and a Welsh pony named Cocotier. Extremely pretty with his perfectly chiseled "Arab-like" head and his mini stallion neck, this black beauty was, first and foremost, a little gangster!

The ponies at my family home worked only during our vacations, a maximum of two hours a day, their whole lives. The rest of the year, they simply enjoyed easy days together in the fields. When I think about them, my heart smiles because I know how happy they were. But if some were happy to see the children arriving for the season of summer camp and tried to take care of their little and often new riders while they were discovering the joy of riding, other ponies were a bit of trouble. Bengal was one of what we called the "Gangster Squad," composed of his father Cocotier, and five others named Kazan, Shapati, Kataclop, Blacky, and Taram.

Cocotier was nicknamed "The Vacuum Cleaner" because when he'd had enough of his young rider, he began tearing at the reins and pulling his nose toward the ground until his small passenger's helmet was completely on his eyes so the child couldn't see anything anymore. Kazan, who was only for the best riders, loved to jump the fence of the arena (which was as high as he was) in order to get back to his friends before the end of the lesson. Shapati had an amazing ability to play sudden practical jokes, such as starting to jump the obstacle in front of her and then changing her mind, letting her rider finish the course alone. Kataclop spent most of his time on two legs (but he switched between the front and the hind so his rider wouldn't get bored with one position). Blacky loved to forget that he had brakes and preferred to race around the ring, his tail like a wild propeller, while Taram deserved an Oscar for his role as a very pretty snail, performing all requested exercises in slow motion—up until the moment he changed gears in one second, and with a big "I got you!" smile on his face, exploded in the air. As soon as his rider was on the ground without even having had the time to realize what just happened, the lazy horse was back, waiting quietly in front of the luckless child with a perfect innocent look that said, "I really have no idea how you got there, kid!"

Oh, yes, I can tell you, the Gangster Squad was a hell of a team, with huge personalities—and that's why we loved them so much.

Bengal's favorite game was to take off at full speed, put his head between his knees, and buck in the air with a back so round it reminded us of a cat asking for cuddles. That's why he was nicknamed "The Toboggan." I can still feel the sensation of riding him in my body! I've never been afraid of falling off a horse, though, and I think I owe this to him and my mother.

As I said, Bengal and I had only a few months of difference in our ages, so he was three and I was four when we started his education. My mum longed him while I rode bareback and tried to stay as still as possible. Many people ask me where my seat on a horse comes from...I think it comes right from those longe lessons! To stay on, I had to go with the flow, to follow Bengal's movement, no matter what. Just "hanging on" would have put me against his rhythm, and I would have had no chance, as obviously he was far stronger and quicker than me. Fluidity was the only answer.

That was the biggest lesson this little gangster taught me, and it is something I have used my whole life, as I've been riding the "complicated" horses ever since—mainly because I wasn't afraid and it was very hard for them to get me off, but also because, since my youngest age, I have always loved to try to find a way forward with the most difficult ponies, the ones everybody was afraid of. I loved the challenge of trying to understand who they were and to find a way to communicate with their strong-mindedness and become their friend. That's what truly thrilled me about riding.

To be honest, I have never been interested in competition. I have been pushed into it, but what I loved, and what I probably miss the most in this professional life where you have to "perform" every single step of the way, was taking the time to tame those who "locked themselves away" from humans. That was the only motivation I needed. We had the sweetest and cutest ponies ever at my family home—the favorite ones of all the camp children who everyone fought to be able to ride. I was never a part of these "battles," as I always fell for the unwanted ponies. My favorites have always been part of some new "Gangster Squad," everywhere I've gone.

With Bengal as a child, on the longe line
and over fences, and as a mother,
with my daughter Louise.

With Shapati.

Shapati
The one who set me free

Shapati was an 11-hand pony of unknown origins, with quite an ugly head, to be honest. But what an incredible personality she had! Mum found her at a food market she went to with my grandmother a few years before I was born. Shapati was there like a piece of meat, a bag of bones, so skinny that the seller was able to put her in the back of the van, grabbing her by her forelock with one hand and by the tail with the other. My mum and grandmother had gone there to buy some vegetables…and came home with Shapati instead! They weren't sure if the small white mare would survive, but leaving her behind wasn't an option.

Not only did Shapati make a full recovery, she became one of the strongest and biggest personalities in the whole stable of ponies, until she died in 2019. She was quite terrible with children, with her very shadow inspiring fear, but

she had an endless gratitude for my mother, which she showed by following Mum everywhere like a dog. She was never taught to do it. That was her, and that was them together. Maybe that loyalty she showed my mother was part of the reason why she stole my heart. I can't say.

I cannot count how many times I fell off Shapati, but it never mattered. I just put my foot back in the stirrup and started again. We still have a very old video of one jumping session where she dumped me 11 times in a row on the same jump! She truly had this unusual and unstoppable technique of starting her jump and then making a 180-degree turn in order to let you finish it alone. When I see this video again, a part of me dies laughing, because it could win an award for the craziest comedy of the year, but another part wonders how I never gave up. I simply went back again, and again, and again, until we eventually finished the obstacle *together*, both on the other side of that oxer! But riding Shapati was like having wings. That's how I will always remember her. She wasn't just "jumping"; she was like a ping-pong ball, and it was a feeling worth all the struggles in the world.

It was the same when we raced in the freshly cut wheat fields. Shapati and I were always the smallest on the start line, and we got even smaller when we took off, as she flattened down a hand or more. But when we reached the finish line, only Sherpa and

my mother might be in front of us; all the others were way behind. To the very end, Shapati was unstoppable, fighting for the victory. I just had to hold tight—my hands in her long thick mane, my shoulders leaning forward in order to follow her speed—and enjoy every single second of it. I vividly remember the sun going down on those late summer evenings, the smell of the dry vegetation of the South of France, and the melody composed by a mix of cicada song, the breath of our ponies, and the rhythm of hooves pounding the ground at full speed. It will forever be my definition of freedom.

We also took the ponies swimming in a canyon that was an hour's hack away from the farm. Most of the time, it actually took us double the time to get there because we were always stopping on our way to grab fruit from the bushes and trees, according to the seasons. Wild cherries, grapes, apricots, blackberries—they were all along our way, and they tasted like heaven.

Once we arrived in the entrance to the canyon, we stopped in the woods and had lunch under the trees and a short nap. Then we put on our swimsuits, jumped on our ponies, and our favorite part of the adventure could start. We had to walk down narrow, steep paths before arriving at *the* spot—a natural water hole about 55 yards long, peacefully waiting for us there, appearing out of nowhere between two cliffs totally incongruous to the typical landscape in the South of France. There, we waited impatiently, one by one, for our turn to go. The ponies knew it, they loved it as much as we did. Holding them back was the biggest challenge! I had to keep Shapati's rump toward the river—otherwise, she was just impossible to keep quiet before our turn. As soon as I gave her the signal, she was full speed, cantering into the water, then starting to swim. I loved that moment coming from extreme powerful speed, water splashing everywhere, hooves crashing into river surface and gravel bottom, until suddenly, everything became smooth, silent, and slow. We were no longer riding ponies then; we were, for a few suspended minutes, the passengers of dolphins.

It is amazing how much these moments are still alive within me, almost 30 years later. They are written in my cells. Although I have had thousands of amazing experiences since my days with Shapati, I don't believe they are as deeply anchored in me as those I've just shared. I can feel myself swimming with Shapati as if it was yesterday. Maybe that's because childhood memories are those of a lifetime. Maybe that's where we define who we will become later on. I have no definitive answer, but I do know that memories of Shapati are the strongest in me, and when I look at how far I have come since then, I realize how much my experiences with her have guided my life and all my choices.

After our swimming excursions, happy as no word can describe, we would sing songs as we rode bareback to a quiet place we knew

*We loved playing in the water
in a beautiful canyon.*

*Riding out with the other campers,
and alongside my mother on Sherpa.*

With Shapati, dressed for an island party
on horseback.

Shapati was the first horse to inspire me
to ride "free," without any tack.

of on top of a hillside. Each of our backpacks contained a bottle of water and a halter and lead rope to attach our ponies to trees as we spent the night together under the stars, rocked to sleep by our ponies' gentle noises.

Time didn't exist. We lived in the moment with an intensity that only children know. Often I dream of rediscovering that ability. It is the biggest gift of life, and one we are sadly losing. Part of it goes when we become adults, but I also think the loss has been more significant since the arrival of internet, social networks, and modern life "on the go." I hope my daughter won't miss out on moments like the ones I had with Shapati because of the new world we are living in. I long for her to also have the chance to experience such intense and wonderful times, because I truly believe that when you eventually have to face the inevitable painful hardships of life, such memories can hold you up and keep you standing in the storm.

Despite her very strong personality, Shapati had a huge heart. She was my partner in some of my very first "show performances," as during each summer camp, my mother and her team worked with all of us (40 children) to put together a big show that we presented to the neighborhood at the end of the month. Shapati was always the one I wanted to ride.

She was also the first horse I ever rode entirely free—without a saddle or bridle—and that's probably what guided me years later, one day in 2014, to remove every piece of tack from my horse Mistral (I share his story on p. 107). I think I was five or six years old when we started playing that game, my mum running in front of us, and Shapati just following her everywhere. It was like we were playing hide-and-seek, and I was just holding on, my sides hurting from laughing. I never thought that something bad could happen. I never felt fear. I never imagined Shapati might just take off, even knowing her quite "spicy" temper. I trusted her and my mother entirely, blindly—to the moon and back. I was *home*. It was our moment. Our very special moment. Something we shared, only the three of us.

Lucky enough to be born in August, my birthdays were always during summer holidays, and there were amazing and magical parties with all the camp children there. My mother and camp staff organized giant "snakes and ladders" games that lasted all day with teams of six engaging in all kinds of activities and "challenges," both with and without our ponies, such as writing songs, playing a "horseball" game, cleaning as much tack as possible in a certain amount of time, identifying food blindfolded, and more. In the evening, after the essential chocolate-raspberry-creamy cake had been eaten, all the teams were reunited around a big campfire for the prize-giving ceremony, followed by each team singing the song they had written.

One special year, as the leader of my team, I chose Shapati as the theme of our song. The tune was from "L'aigle Noir" (the black eagle), sung by the famous French singer Barbara. Our team was to sing our song last, as we had won the game. Normally, we would all—the six of us—sing our song together around the fire, so I don't know why I ended up singing it alone that night. But I do remember closing my eyes while I sang, and when I opened them at the end, seeing tears running down the cheeks of my friends as a very deep silence took over.

I sang that song for many years after that, at the end of every campfire, and I can still remember how it went. They were the very simple words of a little girl, sung to her special unicorn, with whom she shared all her dreams.

Kazan

Kazan

The one who showed me the sky is the limit

Entering his forty-third year of life, Kazan is my living superhero. A bit taller than my earlier ponies, he was, and still is, one of those rare creatures before whom we all bow. He is, like Mistral, made of the stuff of kings. With perfect conformation, both athletic and supple, and an eye sparkling with mischievous intelligence, he was born to lead. If I had to compare him to a human, I would say that he is like Ethan Hunt played by the actor Tom Cruise in *Mission Impossible*. Just last year, at Christmas, when we wanted to catch him in the yard at the farm so we could to put him back in his field for the night, he just jumped the fence, which is as high as him, exactly the same way he did so many times in his youth—effortlessly. We could nearly see the smile on his face when he ran away, full speed, like a young teenager,

proud of how he'd just played us. To me, Kazan is immortal. I honestly don't know how I will handle the day he joins all his friends in heaven.

The first time I got to ride Kazan, I was six years old. It was also during our Christmas vacation. I remember it very clearly. At that time, he was a giant to me. "The Untouchable." The one I dreamed of riding one day. The only one my mother was still riding because he was too wild. Full of blood, with endless energy, his favorite game was to jump the 4-foot fences that surrounded the arena with a terrorized passenger on his back. Once on the other side, he would begin quietly grazing, as if nothing had happened. Only the child crying on his back was a clue to the offense just committed.

I was in awe when I got on Kazan for the first time, but I also felt immediately safe. As with Shapati, being on his back felt like being *home* (I would keep looking for this feeling every time I tried a horse for the rest of my life). Santa Claus had brought me show clothes, so that's how I rode him that day, with me feeling proud, like the Queen of England herself. My mum wasn't exactly relaxed with me on this Ferrari, but Kazan accepted me as his friend that day, and all the days after. We don't know why he behaved like this with me especially, why he took care of me the way he always did. But he did. He was so good he and I even ended jumping a little cross-rail. That was the first time I discovered a horse could fly. The endless

Jumping Kazan showed me a horse could fly.
He made me feel invincible.

power I felt under me every time I had the chance to ride him was something very specific to him. Kazan had wings. Truly.

It was hard because Shapati had taken a huge part of my heart, but Kazan found his way in. They were my two childhood guardian angels. My two best friends. While Shapati taught me the freedom of living the present moment and how to trust my feelings and intuition, Kazan taught me to improve my technique, again and again, in order to become a better rider, until I could free myself from it entirely.

On Kazan's back I truly felt invincible, and I think I was. Being on his back meant becoming fearless, limitless. He was the first horse I jumped 4'6"—it was on the diagonal of our small arena, with straw bales in front. I remember us flying. Together, we were untouchable. He put sparkles in my eyes and butterflies in my stomach.

It was very hard, becoming too tall to ride Kazan and Shapati, and unfortunately, I grew up very fast. By the time I was 10 years old, it was time for me to turn this page. I would give a lot to be able to relive the incredible moments, feelings, and sensations I had with them. They are the real reason why I've been riding horses ever since. In a remarkable parallel, Mistral (my "king") and Sultan (his son), two of the horses of my life, have brought me back to my pony time, each in their own way—and like Kazan and Shapati, my king is dark bay and his son is white.

The competitive experiences I had with Betty opened new doors to me.

Betty Boop
The discovery of the power of adrenaline

When I was nine, I started to ride one time per week at a pony barn (known in France as a "pony club") called *Poneyland d'Antony*. After a trial, I was put straight into the "competition group," and lessons took place on Tuesday evenings from 8:00 p.m. until 10:00 p.m. I was the youngest of the group by far and struggled to keep up with the others at the beginning. I can say it without shame: I was the weakest rider, and sometimes that wasn't easy to take. But as the weeks went by, things started to change, and one day Laurent, our riding teacher, told my mother he wanted to bring me to jumper shows. I wasn't interested in competition, so I refused, but a few months later Laurent came to me at the end of my lesson and asked me what I was doing the following weekend. When I answered

that I didn't know yet, he told me with a big smile that I would be going with him to my first horse show with a pony misnamed "Champion" who everyone hated because he was the ugliest horse in the barn and clearly not the most talented, with quite a strong temper on top of that. But I loved him. Laurent knew that if I got to go with Champion, who was normally not taken to horse shows, I would go, and I did. We ended up third in our class with a clear round, and I was so proud to prove that my ugly Champion deserved more respect than he got.

But while Champion was my overall favorite at the barn, my heart was hypnotized by a strange-looking, chocolate-colored mare measuring almost 13 hands called Betty Boop. Broken under saddle too early, she had never finished her growth properly, and her hindquarters were much higher than her withers, which gave the rider a feeling of being seated on a toboggan headed downhill when you were on her back. At that time, she was feared by all the other riders at the barn because she was extremely fast, not very safe, and could buck in a very violent manner. But she was an incredible jumper.

Laurent had noticed how interested I was in Betty Boop. For the last lesson of the year, just before summer, a trail ride was scheduled. During the allocation of the ponies to each rider in our group, no one wanted to take Betty Boop. I imagined raising my hand, but I didn't dare. I wasn't good enough to ride her. She was only for the tallest and best riders. But Laurent looked at me then and asked if I wanted to ride her. My smile from ear to ear answered him. The other riders and parents present told Laurent he was crazy to allow me to ride her, even more so on a trail ride where the mare was known to be really wild. He replied that I would do very well. The matter was settled. Betty Boop was uncomfortable to ride and I spent the entire two hours trying to stay on as she jumped in the air...but I couldn't stop smiling and I did not fall.

That September, Laurent assigned Betty to another rider (a 14-year-old boy) and to me, for the competition season. I was thrilled. Together, Betty and I were clear and placed in every single start in the jumper ring we took. Betty was a machine. She was fast, agile, quick, and she loved to jump. I had a lot of fun discovering the adrenaline she had and shared with me. I had no goals; there was no pressure. I competed just for fun. I adored the feeling of having to give our best together during one single minute.

Betty Boop and I tried one event together. We were second after dressage and clear after show jumping—but I lost control of my cheetah during cross-country and literally finished in a tree.

Luckily, the fall was more impressive than serious, and it ended only with pretty bruises everywhere.

During late spring, I traveled to the United States for a month and a half with my school, which meant almost certainly losing the chance to qualify for the French Championships that year. To me that wasn't a problem as I never expected to go to the Championships, but Laurent was a bit disappointed about it. The only chance for me to get the last qualifications needed was a competition that took place the day after my return. I arrived at the airport on Saturday, and on Sunday was in the show ring in the last qualifying event for my divisions. To put the odds on our side, Laurent had entered us both in our usual 3'6" (1.10m) division as well as in the one at 3'8" (1.15m). As the qualifier was the Regional Championship, each result counted double. I needed

only one more ranking, so I could afford to end in the middle of the list. The pressure was minimal, especially as Laurent was way more motivated than I was for the qualification. I was jet-lagged but so happy to be back with my special little rocket...and Betty was on fire. She was ready to fight and took me along for the ride. We ended third in our usual division and won the bigger course. That's how we not only qualified for the French Championships, but for the "Elite" Championships, which was a pretty hard event for us to manage at that particular time.

My baby brother was born on the twenty-first of November, 1997—ten years and three months after me. By June of 1998, we were packing all that we owned as we prepared to leave the wonderful little house in the Parisian suburbs in which I had grown up, to live full time in the South of France with our ponies.

This was a huge change. Our "home sweet home" in Arcueil, to name the suburb, had an incredible rosebush with soft pink flowers and a smell like no other. The grandmothers of the village often came to see us when the flowers bloomed to ask us if they might take some. At the back, in our little courtyard, we had a cherry tree that gave us large black fruit at the end of spring. I loved climbing the ladder and eating them long before they had time to reach the basket I was meant to fill. These are memories of a childhood without a shadow in sight. I truly was one of the luckiest and happiest little girls on earth. I loved that little house so much that still, 24 years later, I refuse to pass nearby and see it again. I just can't. I want to keep the memory of it as magical as the real place was for me as a child.

I apologize for this little aside, but it is necessary to help explain the context of my first French Championships. We were leaving my childhood home, we had no hotel, there were boxes stuffed in the car up to the roof, my little brother Morgan was only eight months old, and on top of that, my stepfather (who adopted me officially when I was 20 years old and so became my father) was away, working for six months in China. The family of a friend from the barn had a big bungalow booked near the event site with one bed available, so I ended up spending the week with them and enjoying the swimming pool between classes, while my mother was improvising with Morgan.

That was the first time I discovered the feeling of real stress. When I saw the magnitude of the event, with thousands of ponies and riders, all levels, multiple disciplines, medals, laps of honor…I suddenly realized the challenge Betty and I were facing. I couldn't really eat because my stomach was hurting

like hell. It was time for me to discover this feeling, and it was time for me to start to learn how to handle it. It took me years to tame my nerves, to be honest. It would be the theater that taught me how.

When Betty Boop and I went clear on the first two days, it was hard for me to realize that we had made it to the final and were one of the 20 best. From the 122 combinations on the starting list, we went into the final in seventh place. Another rider was also participating with Betty in the same division, and he didn't qualify. He was very unhappy about the results and told everyone the first day that I only went clear because he went on course first. And the second day he told everyone he had two rails down because Betty was tired from my round. This was another lesson learned for me: I saw how failing a dream can bring very hard feelings and an erroneous view of the situation to convince ourselves that we owe the failure to someone else. It was, I think, my first true step out of my childhood world, and it was very important preparation for the years to come.

In the first round of the final, between the third and the fourth fence, which were a six-stride broken line, my stirrup leather broke. (We would discover after I exited the ring that it had been cut.) Unbalanced, I embarrassed Betty in the approach to the vertical and we had a rail down. But my little kangaroo fought for me until the end of the course, where on the last line, tired from holding on without a stirrup, I asked her to remove one stride so we could just be done! I wasn't disappointed when we left the ring. I was so grateful that Betty had jumped her heart out for me.

In the second round, I had a new stirrup leather in place, and we ended clear. We were in the fight for a medal.

With the recklessness of those trying to accomplish something for the very first time, Betty and I entered our first jump-off together—and won it. I rode the chocolate mare as I had ridden Shapati on the cross-country trails during pony camp, and Betty, with her little ears forward and her unparalleled agility, didn't slow down for a second, flying with the ease of a bird over obstacles that reached the middle of her neck when she stood next to them. I remember seeing tears in my mum and Laurent's eyes. I remember everybody screaming and jumping around. And I remember the very special feeling of adrenaline made of the moments written in the stars.

I rode my little chocolate rocket only for a few months total, but that day, by hoisting me up on an unexpected podium that I had not even dreamed of yet, Betty Boop opened new doors to me. Watching the blue, white, and red flag of my country flutter in the wind, with our national anthem rising in the air while a medal was hung around my neck, and seeing the emotion in the eyes of my mother, first of all, but also everyone else who had encouraged and supported us, made me want to take the adventure further. I had just discovered the taste for competition and victory over oneself. I felt proud of what Betty and I achieved together, in that special moment of that special day.

For a few years in a row after that, that wonderful little mare won several medals with different riders at the French Championships. Despite her weird body, she was a true champion—born to shine, made to win.

Entering another world—these were the horses
who taught me obstinacy, abnegation,
and perseverance. This was the era when
technique took over, leaving behind the joyful
and light world of childhood for the harder,
heavier world of high-level equestrian sport,
with its rules and responsibilities.

Goliat • Foy and Clyde • Ice'n Blue

act II

never give up

With Ice.

IS it not complicated, the time when we have to leave the carefree innocence of childhood and enter adulthood, gradually assuming responsibilities and accepting that the vision we once had of the world must change? Discovering one that is less friendly and more scary?

Goliat, Foy, Clyde, and Ice were my best teachers during the challenging years when I had to establish new guideposts and begin to understand why, for the first time, my emotions sometimes took over. I had been guided only by instinct until then. But now my mind was fighting to lead my heart, and I had to find the balance that would allow both to have a place in my evolution.

I never experienced the phenomenon of anger or desire for revolt that we so often hear about when we discuss adolescence. For me, it was all about *fear*. Fear of failure. Fear of an accident when I suddenly realized that what I was doing could hurt my pony or me. Fear I wouldn't live up to the sacrifices my family made to enable me to perform at the highest level. Fear I would disappoint those who believed in me. Fear I would not *be enough*.

The ponies in this part of my life made me stronger, more tenacious, and taught me one of the lessons I have lived by ever since:

Never give up.

Goliat had model conformation—he was perfectly put together.

Goliat

The one who taught me that relationships aren't to be taken for granted

MY experience with Goliat was the first time I had to realize that relationships can be complicated. My mother bought Goliat for me during the summer following my first French championships. He arrived at the end of August—almost 14 hands, a beautiful fox color, and a body so perfect, he could have been a model for sculptors. He also showed a very good style over the fences for his age, so he was promising.

But Goliat was not made for an 11-year-old girl. He was extremely dominant and very angry at humans. I was his enemy; you could see it in his eyes. As soon as I got on him, his only thought was how to get me off as quickly as possible. I didn't fall off that often, but I have terrible

Goliat was a very challenging horse
on the flat, but once we started jumping,
he was in his element.

memories of him walking on his hind legs, dragging his front legs along the fences of the arena. Some days he would try to catch my leg with his teeth, or just rear and buck with no break, sometimes for a full 30 minutes in a row. At shows, my mum had to take me from the warm-up arena to the competition ring at a trot, holding him without allowing any break before we entered and could go directly into a canter. This was so he wouldn't have a chance to start fighting against me. Always, as soon as we were on the jump course, he went clear and was very easy.

Today I know that Goliat's anger actually came from misunderstandings that occurred when he was started under saddle, but as a green 11-year-old, I didn't yet have much knowledge or experience reading horses, so it t was a very difficult thing for me to accept that a pony or a horse could hate you. Even though the Gangster Squad was full of big personalities and troublemakers, none of them hated their riders. They were playing with the children, laughing at them, being a bit naughty, being scoundrels, but in the end, it was always good-natured and without resentment

Goliat would run to me when I visited him at his new barn,
but I could never forgive him entirely.

or real bad intention. With Goliat, though, I came to understand that some horses were not made to become your friend.

The weirdest part of his story is that Goliat actually became the easiest pony to be around later on. He was a "winning machine" and super-safe—all the riders fought to ride him. I had grown suddenly after just a short while with him, reaching 5'7" in only a few months, and he became too small for me, so we leased him out. I often visited the stable where he was to help his riders when they were struggling a bit. Every time I arrived at the barn when he was out in the field, he neighed and ran toward me. His riders (two sisters) and their coach always said that Goliat only did this with me, no matter how many months since I'd last seen him, and that it showed how much he was bonded to me, how much he respected me, and I want to believe that was true. But my heart could never love him back. I built a wall between us. I respected him, and I recognized his talent and the truly great pony he eventually became, but I couldn't forget the "other Goliat"—the one who had made me go through hell. The one who, for an entire year, had made me cry each time I rode him due to incomprehension, sadness, and sometimes even fear. I was still too young to understand all this. For me, it seemed normal to expect for him to accept me on his back since in my eyes, "riding" and "being ridden" was just a shared game. I didn't see it as a task or job that could be unpleasant for him. Later on in my journey, my understanding changed, of course, but at that time of my youth, even though Goliat and I eventually overcame these difficulties together, I could not forgive him entirely for what he had put me through.

Today I know and can say just how important he was in my development as a rider and horseperson, and how important the life lessons he taught me were. I am grateful to him for being a part of my journey.

Foy had a very thin, light build—like a small horse, rather than a pony.

Foy and Clyde

The two opposites who propelled me into adulthood

When I was 12, after my dramatic growth spurt, my parents were approached one day following the awards ceremony at a show by a person who had a very difficult but extremely talented mare who the person thought might fit me very well. We weren't in the position to buy a horse at the time, so we didn't follow up for several months. Then one day, in November, the mare's owner called us again to say that we should really come and try her. She was in Spain, ridden by a professional adult rider, about three hours' drive from us. As I had been homeschooled since we left Paris, it was easy to organize a visit. That's how we discovered Foy, an Anglo-Arab who had stayed "pony size" because she had been born with a twin.

Foy was super thin with long gazelle legs, a rather weird face with a bump on her nose, some very long and flat ears, and what seemed like three curly hairs in place of a forelock. I rode her for the first time very early on a frozen morning. The sun was shining and the light was wonderful. What I felt under the saddle that day was completely different than anything I had ever felt before. She moved like a *horse*. The movements felt enormous and less elastic. Everything seemed unstable. I had no benchmark anymore. On top of that, Foy spent the first 15 minutes hopping around like a jackrabbit.

But when we started jumping, it felt like a dream. Foy had an incredible "punching" energy in the last stride before she jumped. She could switch from 2-foot stride to a 13-foot stride in a second. I was riding a Ferrari and just trying to be up to the task.

We ended jumping a course with no hole left on top of the standards. I had never *ever* jumped that high in my life. We were over 4"6" (1.40m), and it looked easy for her, even though she was under 15 hands. Of course, I got off the mare with stars in my eyes and my heart pounding. I was on a little cloud, amazed, ecstatic. But she was too expensive when we considered how difficult she was as well as our budget. My mother was understandably concerned about Foy's well-known difficult temperament after our experience with Goliat.

However, about a month later, on New Year's Eve, Foy's owner called us to offer the mare for half the price...and that was the beginning of a new big chapter in my horse life.

I remember my mother hanging up the phone, turning to me and asking if I was sure I wanted Foy when she was known to be a particularly difficult mare. I answered yes. Mum wanted me to be truly involved in the choice and to take responsibility for it, so my parents told me they would pay two-thirds of the money, and the last part would have to come from me. I had an account that had been opened by my paternal grandmother in my name when I was six years old to help compensate for the fact that my biological father never took care of me and never gave a penny to my mother to help her raise me. The money was intended to help me pay for my studies at university later on. So using it to help pay for Foy was my first big decision in life, and being a part owner of her became my first true responsibility.

Foy was a mare that could not be counted on. She had constant ups and downs, and her moods were extremely changeable. Sometimes she filled me with euphoria as I enjoyed her athleticism, power, and strength. Sometimes she filled me with despair, as she became entirely inaccessible and offered me nothing. She could jump 4'6" (1.40m) one day and categorically refuse to pass over a ground pole the next, making a huge drama out of it with crazy eyes and theatrical reactions. Showing her was the same. At our first and only French Championships, we won the first round of qualification after a terrible warm-up, and the day after, she was incredibly relaxed in the warm-up and then wouldn't even approach the first fence on course. (At age 28, Foy still made life difficult for others as she ruled over the otherwise peaceful retirees with whom she shared a meadow at a close friend's place in Normandy, directing everyone and only letting them eat with her permission. This earned her the nickname of "The Terrible Grandma." She died in 2023, at age 29.)

With her horse-like locomotion and Thoroughbred temper, Foy challenged me to a new dimension of riding. I had to learn, progress, and understand very quickly, because she was not a horse with a forgiving nature. The slightest technical error had immediate repercussions. She made this very clear. At the same time, since she had enough energy for an entire

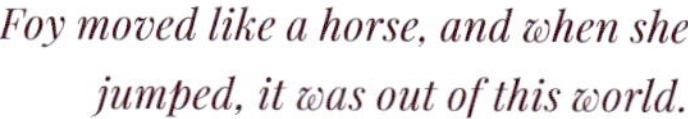

Foy moved like a horse, and when she
jumped, it was out of this world.

army and was never tired, she allowed me to use what I had
learned about balance and seat when riding Bengal bareback on
the longe line. The only possible answer when Foy twisted and
turned in the air for several minutes in a row without stopping,
while I barely had a foot in a stirrup, was to stay calm and un-
flappable, and patiently wait for the storm to pass. You couldn't
get into a fight with her, because while she was indeed a very
dominant personality, she was also ultra-sensitive.

Foy and her genius jumping style opened doors for me that
I never imagined. One day I accompanied a friend of mine,
Charlotte, when she was invited to a clinic with the brand-new
French National Pony Show Jumping Team Trainer, Marcel
Delestre. Charlotte refused to go alone, and I was of course
very excited and super happy to join her, but I didn't really

understand how important the day could be. To me it was just
a beautiful experience and the chance to train once with a very
well-known horseman.

I guess it is exactly because I didn't understand what was
at stake that I was able to ride totally relaxed and without any
pressure. Foy had a big day. Those who were there could see only
her and think, "Holy shit! What is *that*?" She had no break point,
no limit—just like my smile.

At the end of the clinic Marcel Delestre asked my mother if
I could come to Lamotte-Beuvron where the French Equestrian
Federation was hosting a training camp during the Christmas
holidays. He was inviting 10 pony-and-rider combinations to be
part of another clinic, this time to prepare for the upcoming
international season.

Everything moved quickly from that day, and by the middle of January 2002, Foy and I were participating in our first international pony show jumping competitions together. Was it that I was entering adolescence and experiencing the loss of innocence that goes with it? Was it the complicated financial situation and my parents making big sacrifices in their lives so I had a chance to compete at an elite level and accept the responsibilities that went along with it? Was it suddenly an awareness of the physical risks and the danger when jumping such high fences with increasing technical difficulty? I can't say exactly the cause, and I honestly think it was a mixture of all that, but what's certain is that I went through two extremely formative but difficult and painful years. For the first time, I struggled with self-doubt and the fear of disappointing.

I was incredibly proud of representing my country and defending our colors. I clearly remember the speech we got during that first team clinic, which explained to us the model behavior that we had to have, the exemplarity that we had to represent, and the values of hard work, self-improvement, self-control, respect, loyalty, and perseverance that we had to embody. These words resonated in me so strongly that I made it my life to be disciplined and live up to the Federation's expectations. I locked myself in this "straitjacket" for several years, losing sight of the real reason why I love being with horses so much—the freedom they give us, and the pleasure inherent in the constant search to understand a fascinating animal whose language we do not speak.

I was focused—and I needed to be focused—on improving my technique, but it made me lose my instinct for a while. I was just about to discover that the greatest enemy of the rider is doubt, because to doubt—beyond the technical problems that go hand in hand with it—is to betray your horse. You can doubt before getting in the saddle. You can doubt after you get off. We can and we all do make mistakes, every single day. But to doubt when you ask something of your horse is to put him in a position of weakness and discomfort, which is much worse than the resulting error itself. It took me a while to truly understand that, and even more time before I was able to put it into practice.

Foy was a genius, but she was very unstable. Today, with my experience and knowledge, I think we could have helped her maybe with natural hormonal balancing products. It could have made a difference. But this depth of knowledge came far later. Becoming a horseman takes a whole lifetime. You never stop learning. You never stop growing. That was not my story with Foy. She was on my path to teach me many other things, such as precision, nuance, self-control, self-questioning, and perseverance.

Foy didn't forgive me the slightest mistake. It was her rule. I was never the leader with her. I was too young, too inexperienced to know. I was impressed by my phenomenal mare with her explosive temper. Being with her was a mix of different feelings I had to discover and learn how to handle. Some were fantastic. Others were very painful. Ours wasn't a peaceful relationship. It was a passionate relationship between a teenager and a very special chestnut princess. I admired her incredible personality (believe me or not, she was "talking" to me all the time when I was on her, which helped me be prepared for whatever was coming next). I feared her changing moods and her excessive and unpredictable outbursts of anger. I loved her terribly for those very special moments when, finally, we were *one.* In those moments, the whole world stopped spinning because the sensations she offered me were

unparalleled. I hated her for never needing me, never caring for me, never really letting me in. Foy was a loner and a leader who needed no one but herself. Sometimes she chose to let me or another horse enter her "bubble" for a while, but she dictated the terms of the relationship.

In June 2002, Marcel was frustrated by how unreliable Foy was despite being such a big talent. He decided to ride her in order to try to help me. We were in Switzerland, 24 hours before the veterinary check of our next international competition. From the moment Marcel sat on her back, you could see the monumental anger simmering in Foy's eye. She was outraged. After an eventful warm-up but still under control, Marcel called for the first jump. I remember setting it with my mum. It was a cross-rail; a very small one. But in her rage, Foy took off from a distance that didn't exist, and both horse and trainer crashed to the ground. I can still feel in my body the shock of seeing them both down and the silence that followed.

Marcel got up of the ground, but he didn't get back on her. I went to catch Foy where she was cantering free in the arena; Marcel left us without a glance.

During the next three days of competition, I could not persuade Foy to go farther than the first fence. Even in the warm-up, she refused to go. I don't even know why I tried. I think I still had a little spark of hope, but it was totally in vain. I was desperate, helpless, hopeless, and felt completely alone as Marcel didn't speak one word to me on that terrible weekend. I felt abandoned, left on the side of the road, guilty of a fault that I hadn't committed.

It was a day that marked a definitive breaking point for Foy, from which she never recovered. If, over time, I was able to do big courses again at home, with ease and pleasure, far from the pressure of competition, I was never able to finish a class on her thereafter. I tried twice, but the stress Foy experienced meant it didn't make sense at all anymore.

It wasn't the end of our story together, but it was the end of our competitive journey. A hard one. I was 14, and for the first time, my dream was collapsing and my entire world with it. I had been doing school at home on my own, training ponies in the morning, and working in the afternoons. I had a plan; I had a goal; I knew where I was heading. And suddenly, everything was over. I also discovered the jealousy and wickedness that sometimes resides in those who dream to be in your place but never will. I was not prepared for it. I felt dirty, empty, and endlessly sad when I saw people elated and giving each other high fives with beaming smiles on their faces because Foy and I had failed. I couldn't understand this reaction in others. It left a deep scar within me and created a certain mistrust of people. Luckily, my family offered the support and protection I needed. They helped me get through the difficult emotions I was experiencing and accept them as part of life when you choose to push your limits and reach for your dreams.

A few weeks after the Swiss incident, Marcel called my mother to tell her that a very good pony was for lease. He knew we couldn't afford it and had already warned the owners, who had received several big offers, but he had convinced them that I was the right match for the mare named Clyde. And Clyde's owners were not like so many others. Passionate breeders beyond words, what they wanted most was the story of their pony and her human partner to be beautiful...and that's what it became.

Clyde was the exact opposite of Foy. She was a very heavy white Connemara mare with solid bones and an even temper. Just thinking of her makes me smile—she was funny, happy, and an amazing friend.

Where Foy was energy at a permanent boil, Clyde was a quiet force, with energy too, but in a completely different way. She was smart, good-natured, joyful, a pranker. Apart from food (namely carrots and apples), her favorite thing was when I was scratching her belly. She almost fell over during this ritual more than once. When she saw me coming, she would raise her hind leg in order to notify me that, before anything else, she had to have her scratches. You can't even start to imagine the facial expressions she made with her nose during these special moments. She was a clown, a real one, a touching one. I loved her immediately. Beneath her chubby Connemara exterior, she had a huge and ultra-sensitive heart. She had, of course, a temper of her own (you better not have to compete during lunch time, or she would be extremely grumpy and upset in the ring!), but she was, above all, my friend, truly.

Technically, Clyde had an enormous strength. The feeling was something new and different for me. After the ultra-quickness of Foy, Clyde was a super-powerful, slow-motion jumper. We started out together quite well, quickly finding success.

It was at this time that I first discovered what real pressure was. People were watching us, waiting for us to succeed—or fail. Marcel was counting on us. I wasn't just part of the French Team anymore, I was one of its leaders. It was also the beginning of social media's presence in our lives, and I was confronted with what it was like to have people commenting on your riding but also on your life, without even knowing you. I have no shame in saying that I didn't know how to manage this pressure at that time, and I didn't cope with it well.

In the middle of the season, just before our first Nations Cup, Clyde and I had a terrible show in Fontainebleau. The first day went quite well, as we were clear until nearly the end of the course, but the last jump was an oxer with a large ditch in the ground below, filled with pebbles. The distance came perfectly—I saw it with plenty of time, but my gray champion saw the hole under the jump at the last minute and got scared. I jumped the oxer quite well…but alone.

The day after, the same obstacle was Fence 4, and while I didn't fall, Clyde refused twice, and we were eliminated. We started the Grand Prix anyway, with the same issue at the same fence once again.

This can always happen with horses, of course, but I had put so much pressure on myself to live up to Marcel's expectations, the owner's trust, and my family's hopes that I was completely destroyed after that weekend. On Tuesday we had to drive to Diest, in Belgium, for the Nations Cup. I felt like I didn't deserve that chance anymore. I was afraid of disappointing and betraying my team by not being up to the task. I remember crying the whole day Monday. It was Easter. My family organized an egg hunt at our bed-and-breakfast, but the tears flowed; I couldn't hold them back. My little brother, five at the time, tried his best to make me smile and cheer me up. He was so cute, so caring, so present by my side. (He still is, 20 years later. He is one of my pillars of strength.)

That evening, Mum called Marcel to tell him that I wasn't ready to go to Diest, which was to be the hardest competition I had ever done before. But he answered that he still trusted me to defend France's colors in Belgium and that he wouldn't replace us. I am very grateful to him for what he did that day, because he could have easily replaced me on the team. Many others hoped for my spot. By supporting me through my first really big competitive failure, which marked me so deeply, he gave me a great life lesson: You can fall one day and get up stronger the next. Failure is part of the journey; it is inevitable. Even more, it is necessary for your construction and your evolution. Failure allows us to take a breath, to regain our strength. The truth is, we are rarely built on our successes but mainly through our failures, the obstacles placed on our path, and the difficult times we must go through. Marcel's trust was everything I needed to get back on my feet and stand up tall again.

Clyde and I ended being the best combination of the team at the Nations Cup on Saturday, and a bit tired at the end of the Grand Prix on Sunday, we had two rails down. But from our low point

just five days before, the result was more than I could have hoped for. While the weekend before I had discovered how people could be mean and jealous sometimes, calling Clyde's owners immediately after our elimination in an effort to get her for themselves, in Belgium I discovered for the first time what true team spirit is like and the friendships that can result from it. For five days, we stuck together and supported each other in our joys and in our sorrows. For me, *this* is equestrian sport. It is a search for self-transcendence, but above all, it is a respect between athletes that increases the flow of adrenaline and positive emotions tenfold. The Nations Cup was the first time I really experienced that kind of camaraderie, and it was even more important to me because since my family's move to the South of France, I had been doing my schooling on my own at home. I was alone most of the time, surrounded by animals, and I loved it. But this "team feeling" also felt amazing. It was like being carried along by a synergy that made you a thousand times stronger.

Clyde and I continued our season with ups and downs. I had trouble managing my emotions and doubt sometimes won its battle, causing me to make mistakes in my riding. But even with my slip-ups, we were on the "long list"—the last eight combinations—in the running for selection for the European Championships. The last step was the French Championships.

Unfortunately, the morning we were to depart for the determining competition, we found Clyde lying down in her stall, injured after a very unusual wasp attack. As she had fought

Clyde jumped with incredible power,
and we clicked immediately.

Experiencing what it was like to be part of a real team of riders who supported each other was an amazing opportunity for me, as I spent so much time alone or just with my ponies.

against the insects, she had cut both her elbows with her metal shoes. The veterinarian came and treated her injuries, and considering what was at stake, told us to go ahead to the Championships and give it a try. We called Clyde's owners and asked what they thought, and they said the same thing.

At the show, Clyde jumped as she never did. The pictures of the three first fences show her a foot over the top poles. But when the water jump came, the spread tugged at her wounds, and she stumbled on the landing, refusing to go on to the triple that was coming next. I understood immediately and didn't even ask her to continue. I raised my hand, and we left the arena.

That's how our race for the European Championships brutally ended. Strangely, the sadness and disappointment I felt were not the same as they had been in Fontainebleau, probably because this time, it was no one's fault. It was fate. We couldn't predict it. We couldn't know. Accepting it was the only possible answer.

What made me terribly sad, on the other hand, was the separation that was to come—I had to let go of the clown-faced mare to whom I had become so attached. But once again, her owners refused money and said they preferred to leave Clyde with me, even if I had aged out of competing her. We found a young girl who leased her and rode her on the weekends. During the week, I continued to train her. She stayed with me

until it was time for her to retire at her farm and make babies. She died in her field, age 27, while I was far away. When I got the news, I hadn't seen her in a while, as hundreds of miles were between us, but the pain was huge. Clyde didn't give me exactly the competitive success we had all hoped for when our story together started. No, she taught me much more. She taught me things that help me every single day in my adult life—about myself, about emotions, about solidarity, and about the deep bond that can unite people around one dream. The very special and difficult year I shared with her is filled with memories deeply rooted in me that often resonate in my daily life. I grew a lot by her side. She is the one who, when I was 15, brought me into adulthood. It was time for me to enter yet another world, and it was my competitive season with her that left me with a taste of unfinished business that would decide my fate a few years later. While high-level competition was certainly not my ultimate goal, I still had the feeling of not having finished what I had started. The diehard and driven part of me remained unsatisfied, while the artistic and ethereal part was pushing me to leave everything I knew behind and join a professional theater school, which I did next, when I turned 16 years old.

With Ice.

Ice'n Blue

The outsider who changed the whole game

I was a very happy and fulfilled teenager as I pursued acting and had the chance to play all sorts of roles on stage, when Clyde's owners called me during the summer of 2004. They asked if I would like to present their stallion Ice'n Blue to Laurence Sautet, the trainer of the French National Pony Dressage Team at that time. I didn't know their stallion, and all I knew about dressage was what I was doing on my own as I trained my jumping ponies. It was true that my teammates had nicknamed me "The Dressage Rider" because I liked to do leg-yields and flying changes up to every two strides during my warm-up before a jumping round, but I had no academic understanding of dressage technique at all. I tried things only out of curiosity and fun at first, and continued to use them when

I found them very useful and complementary for the training I was doing over jumps.

Well, I entered the "arena of honor" at the famous Cadre Noir of Saumur, one of the most prestigious classical riding schools in the world, in a jumping saddle with my stirrups extended by seven holes, on the back of a small white stallion with a neck as round as his head was finely chiseled, who I had only ridden three times in my life. We tried our best. Ice was a true sweetheart, as pretty inside as outside. He had a very nice and uphill canter and a correct walk, but his trot was a bit too "average" for international competition. Laurence, therefore, decided not to retain him for the Team.

A very tall figure all dressed in black had watched me ride from his office overlooking the arena. It was Philippe Limousin, member of the Cadre Noir, and trainer of the French Juniors and Young Riders Teams. When Ice and I had finished, he came to Laurence to say that I was talented, but Laurence answered that I was too old for the pony divisions. Philippe then asked me to come to a "Young Talent" scouting clinic scheduled for three weeks later and only an hour away from our home in the South of France. I answered that I had left the equestrian world for the theater, and I had no horse. The conversation, however, awakened in me a feeling of regret that I had never participated in a European Championship.

After we had left, Ice's owner asked if I would like to take him home with me so I could ride in the clinic, and in the meantime, prepare the pretty stallion for a pony rider. This was how, with one foot in the theater in Marseille and another back in a stirrup in Canaules, I presented myself at the scouting event in Saint Martin de Crau a month later. For the occasion, I had also transformed Clyde into a "dressage pony"—a game to which she had lent herself with maximum effort and her enormous, always-happy heart.

This clinic would set me on a career path that I did not want, but which was clearly my destiny. Philippe asked me again what I wanted to do with my life. My answer was the same: I wanted to be an actress. But this time, his reply to me was different. He said, word for word, "You have plenty of time to play characters on stage. Come and do some dressage first. Then you will have all the time in the world to play the clown."

And that was how I returned to the equestrian world. Philippe's words deflected my journey, for better and for worse. Often, I wonder what I might have become if his words hadn't gotten under my skin, but the truth is, I will never know.

Ice stayed with me until the following summer. The deal was that I was to compete him in national-level pony Grand Prix competitions to prepare him for a "real" pony rider. It would also allow me to gain experience in the dressage arena. The first time we competed, I remember I didn't even know how to enter the arena, when I had to start my test, or how to salute the judges. Ice and I were alone, with my mum helping but not knowing any better than I did. In the warm-up I was on my own, sneaking looks at the other riders in order to try and do it all right. I discovered that boots and wraps were forbidden, my pony's braids were

Schooling Ice at home to prepare him for
his dressage career was a joy. Just as I used
the little dressage I knew with my jumping ponies,
I sometimes jumped Ice to mix things up.

absolutely terrible, and my outfit was not quite the latest in dressage fashion—but as my grandmother often told me, "You can't make an omelet without breaking eggs." Everything was so different from what I was used to. I was lost, and Ice was inexperienced. But we learned on the job together, getting better every time, observing those around us. I think I can say Ice was my partner in breaking eggs, and he got me through. We ended up participating in the French Pony Grand Prix Championships and finished middle of the class, with no shame but no shine either.

Ice allowed me to learn, search, discover. I had a whole new world of sensations, feelings, movements, and understandings opening up to me. He helped me push open the doors to dressage, and I am truly grateful to him for his kindness, his bonhomie, and his sweet heart.

Unfortunately, Ice died way too early, only a couple of years after our time together, at the farm where he was born, following a terrible colic. His owners sent a text message to my mother so she could prepare me for the terrible news, but unfortunately, I saw it as I was taking the phone to her, and I remember a feeling of incomprehension, followed by a great emptiness. My first thought was that I must have misread. My brain was not ready to accept what my eyes had registered.

Ice was a shooting star, and if you look up in the sky, on a clear night, I'm sure you will see his light shining through.

Welcome to the dressage world,
where I discovered new sensations,
new movements, and learned further to control
my own body in order to be able to *pretend*
to control the balance of my dancing partners.

Lambrusco • Donatello • Joeris

act III

learning
to stand
strong

I had other plans. I wanted to be an actress, an author, and eventually, a film director. I was born for it. My thoughts have always been entangled in telling powerful stories, creating magical worlds, bringing dreams to life. But sometimes fate gets involved.

I took the turn of life I describe ahead when I was seventeen, thinking that it would be an "aside" of three years maximum where I would push myself and open myself to a new challenge, discover new feelings and experiences on horseback, and keep going until the natural end of my story with high-level equestrian sport. In the end, this "Act" in my life lasted for ten years.

I owe it to the passionate people who made me fall in love with the eternal quest for perfection that is inevitably linked to dressage. But I owe it even more to the amazing schoolmasters I had the chance to meet during my journey. These horses enabled me to discover how powerful a simple perfect stride can be and the emotion it can make you feel during that very special stolen second.

During these years, it was like being a blank page again, starting from zero, not knowing where I was heading, but following the rhythm of the horses in my life. Living day by day. Learning by their sides, again and again. Dedicating myself entirely to them and the lessons they were teaching me. Trying to understand as well as I could the thousands of pieces of information they gifted me, even when I did not know yet what I would do with it. Setting new goals.

This part of my life was not an easy journey. I had to go through tough moments and learned lessons sometimes the hard way. No big changes in life are easy. That scenario doesn't exist. But these horses made me stand on my own two feet. They made me show up again every time I had one knee down, ready to give up. They made me overcome physical pain with mental strength. And Donatello taught me to fight for what I believed (and still do!) was the right thing to do.

With Lambrusco.

Lambrusco

The one who made it all possible

I was presenting Ice at a stallion show during a horse fair in November of 2004, accompanied by my friend Camille, when she and I saw a beautiful horse pass by. As I stared, quite amazed by his special beauty, Camille told me she knew his rider, and motioned for me to follow her toward the pair. After greeting the horse's rider, Mustapha, and introducing me, Camille rather jokingly said, "Do you happen to have a horse to lend Alizée, by chance? The trainer of the Junior Team has scouted her and wants her to come to the Christmas camp in Saumur, but she doesn't have a horse."

Although it started just as a joke, in true fairytale fashion, Mustapha jumped down, and asked me to go ahead, get on, and show him what I could do.

The sculptural bay had a double bridle on. I had only ridden two or three times in my life with one but pretended I was used to it. *The show must go on.* Lambrusco was the horse's name, and he was a pure beauty, but he was extremely stiff, and I struggled to keep my seat in the saddle. After my short ride on him, I felt pain in every single part of my body, especially in my abdominals and adductors, but I was very grateful and happy to have had the chance to live such an experience—to have been able to ride a "real" dressage horse, in a real dressage saddle, and to have been able to feel amazing new sensations. When I got off, I was hurting all over, but I was smiling ear to ear. I was very curious to hear what Mus, who had let me ride his horse on my own for a good half hour, might recommend for finding a horse. To my extreme surprise, then and there he offered me the opportunity to come to his house three days a week and continue to ride Lambrusco in preparation for the training camp in Saumur, which was to take place in five weeks' time. My family did not have a lot of money to pay him, but Mus wanted to dream along with us. It was an unlikely encounter—one that you usually only see in movies.

During the weeks that followed, I spent half my time at his family's bed and breakfast, which was closed to customers at that time of the year, so I had a place to stay. I helped Mus and his wife in the barn in the morning, then I rode Lambrusco ("Coco") and also Gibraltar, a giant gray with a big heart, who was more advanced in his dressage work but whose gaits weren't good enough to ride him in the clinic. Mus gave me as much information and advice as he could in such a short time. It was an accelerated training. He was as passionate as he was impatient. He wanted me to *get there.* The project had become his pet. He put his whole heart into it.

I owe Mus a lot for this time—beyond the loan of his horse, his saddle, his bridle, and his horse trailer. I haven't had enough opportunities to thank him publicly for what he did for me, when I was nothing and nobody, coming out of nowhere. On a November day when we were chilled by the cold mistral blowing through the Montpellier exhibition center, he decided not only to believe in me, but also to give everything he had to make my dream happen, without ever asking anything else in return other than for me to fight for the chance to wear the French colors in the international dressage arena. He also had this dream, for himself, but he knew he would not achieve it for various reasons. "Live my dream—that's my biggest reward." That's what Mus always told me whenever I said I didn't know how to thank him for all he was doing. He was by our side when we went to Saumur for our first team training

where we got a chilly welcome from the other riders and their parents because I came from the jumping world. He was with us during our first Junior Team test, which was an absolute disaster.

Unfortunately, Lambrusco's health wasn't perfect, and we were too short in time. The wonderful dark bay had been treated for back weakness several times before I met him, and after a few months, he started to seem a bit uncomfortable again. Together with Mus we decided it was better for Coco to return to the South of France, where I know he lived happily until his last breath.

But I owe Coco my first pirouettes, my first "real" extended trot, my first true dressage journey. He was the first horse to allow me to feel that with the proper work, aids, and energy, I could modify the rhythm, the cadence, and the amplitude of the trot, and that a seemingly "ordinary" horse could become extraordinary.

He opened the doors to a world that I had not yet imagined. It was only the very beginning. I was still far from understanding to what extent dressage could be a quest for the Holy Grail, for surpassing ourselves, for aiming for the same perfection of movement as a dancer at the barre.

Coco and I hadn't really the time to build a true relationship—we only had about five months together, during which I had to learn so much technique in such a short time that I was primarily focused on just trying to understand everything well enough so as not to disturb him. But we both gave our best to each other.

In the end, Mus and I did not achieve our shared dream together; life had other plans. But I started to compete internationally the following year, and I would never have done it without him... and sweet Coco.

Donatello became my everything.

Donatello
My first heartbreaker

How to start with Donatello? How to describe this dark chocolate giant with such an enormous shining aura? Donatello is a very special story. I rode him only a few months of my life, but they were very intense, and they changed me forever.

It begins when I met one of Mus's closest friends, Didier, and he offered me the ride on an energetic chestnut mare named Gaufrette in order to be able to enter the three-year course at the Cadre Noir in Saumur.

I had just finished school, graduating with honors, and even though a part of me was still very thirsty to learn more, to push my studies further, and to return to the theater, another part was attracted by a potential adventure in such an emblematic equestrian place, at the time still led by the charismatic

Philippe Limousin, who pushed me to pursue dressage a bit longer. For the second time of my short life, I chose the path offered by this 6'6" 60-year-old with his tenor voice and eagle eyes. But Gaufrette didn't really fit the profile expected by Philippe, and Didier had clients interested in buying her, so our story ended after only a few months. I rode up to 12 horses a day—school horses and others—but I no longer had a real partner to build a new story with.

Then Fabien, our dressage instructor at the Cadre Noir, came to me one day and offered me the chance to ride Donatello, his Grand Prix horse, sometimes. The funny thing is that during my very first competition with Lambrusco, I had noticed Fabien and Donatello in the warm-up, and my heart had missed a beat. Donatello was a colossus with a pony heart. On that day that I remembered, he was jumping in the air, and he even managed to jump the arena fence during the Grand Prix. That was him. A wild and incredible soul. That's what I loved so much about him. When I got on him for the first time, I had sparkles in my eyes and butterflies in my belly. I nearly felt out of control after crossing the arena without ever having all four feet on the ground, but it didn't matter at all. I was on a cloud. Donatello instantly became my whole world. It was love at first ride.

I started riding "Doudou" first once a week, then twice, then four times—and then I had full responsibility for him, and those were my happiest days. Fabien and Donatello did not suit each other. One was a talented obsessive perfectionist. The other was an artist with the spirit of an uncontrollable child who refused to be locked into any straitjacket. After several years together, the dialogue between Fabien and Donatello was over. They had no more friendship. No more understanding. Fabien recognized that the big horse and I could have a special bond.

We were two hearts on edge, highly sensitive, with trouble fitting into the picture expected of us.

Doudou suddenly became my reason to be, to get up in the morning, to ride the other horses, to work hard. My life had meaning because of him. He became my everything. It was something I'd never felt before. The feeling overturned everything in its path and illuminated my days with a new light. An immense serenity took hold of me. I didn't know where we were going. I didn't know what the future would be. We had no specific goal together. But I had Doudou, and that was enough for me.

The big horse paid me back. He was known at Saumur for his grumpy and unpleasant temper, but he always greeted me with his ears forward and a little raspy neigh. For me, Doudou was the most perfect horse on earth. I always first went to see him in the morning before the day started, then spent my lunch breaks with him, and came back to him once my days were over and the stables completely empty. Jimmy, his appointed groom at the time, was always grumbling about Donatello and his "pig-like character" and temper tantrums. He truly adored Doudou, even if he bitched about him, and liked to join us at lunchtime and chat with me while I took care of my soulmate. One day, as he teased me as usual, saying how terrible Donatello's temper was, and as I once again came to the horse's defense, Jimmy suggested that we do a little test to see who was right. I hid in a corner of the barn while Jimmy walked past Donatello's stall, whistling. The big horse popped his head out, ears flat and mouth gaping, pretending to attack, as he did most of the day with everybody passing by, it was true. Then Jimmy and I switched roles, so that I walked in front of Doudou's box, calling him. As always with me, he stuck his head out, ears forward, neighing in that broken voice that was his.

Everything was said. Doudou and I had found each other.

One day I broke my piggy bank to buy Donatello a magnificent Baker plaid blanket. I was so happy that I went to put it on him that very evening. The next morning, when I arrived at the stable, I told Jimmy about it, still feeling proud and excited.

Jimmy turned pale and exclaimed, "You didn't leave it on him overnight, did you?"

"Of course I did," I answered.

I then watched Jimmy run toward Doudou's stall, saying that in the 10 years he had taken care of him, no blanket had survived Donatello more than three hours. The horse hated them.

Prepared for the worst when Jimmy opened the door, me right on his heels, we found a perfectly innocent Doudou, his new blanket still in place, looking at us as if to say, "What's the problem here?" It remained a private joke between Jimmy and me.

We made a nice trio together.

Fabien understood very quickly the special bond that was born between Doudou and me. He asked that Donatello, who was not only his Grand Prix horse but also his solo horse for the famous "Galas," or public shows, of the Cadre Noir, be assigned to me. Even if Doudou officially remained "his" horse, it was now clear to everyone that it was I who was actually in charge of him. Although later on Fabien and I had major disagreements about Donatello, I will still be forever grateful to him for everything he taught me, for the incredible opportunity he gave me, and for the amazing moments we shared, the three of us. With Donatello and Fabien I discovered sensations I would forever try to reproduce later on: my first tempi changes, my first real Grand Prix pirouettes, my first steps of passage. They allowed me to discover that dressage, when well done, is a ballet where the effort is not seen— only bodies, speaking to each other. They made me understand how a horse can have the power of a giant and the lightness of a feather. They showed me the magic of when, finally, the movement becomes perfect, suspended in the air, simple and fluid. I owe them both what would become my continuous quest later in my life: that moment when the most technically difficult movements suddenly become nothing more than a game, because two bodies and minds align to form one, working with a complete synergy, each with a perfect understanding of the other. That's when riding becomes a dance; that's when the horse becomes confident and proud; that's when you close your eyes, hoping to never wake up.

The few months we first spent together were a golden parenthesis, a pause in time. Donatello and Fabien made me take a huge technical leap forward. They allowed me to really elevate to another level of riding skill and understanding of the dressage discipline. Because my wonderful chocolate-colored partner never forgave me anything and took advantage when I didn't ask him for a movement the right way, and because Fabien invested immense energy, patience, and benevolence in us, our work sessions were sacred moments for me that I would not have missed for anything in the world. But beyond this technical and educational aspect, there was also this feeling of having created a cocoon, a blended family of sorts. Inside was grumpy, big-hearted Jimmy, Fabien (who under his haughtiness actually hid hypersensitivity), and Donatello, this colossus with an extraordinary personality. And then there was me who, surrounded by these three beings, was the happiest I had ever been in the world. I had found my place of balance.

After a few national competitions, Philippe asked Fabien to register us for the international competition in Le Touquet, and Donatello gave me my very first international victory there. What you feel with that first hymn that resonates...that pride. I was on a cloud, surrounded by people I liked very much, by the side of the most extraordinary horse I'd ever met. Only my family was missing, but they crossed the whole of France to be by our side in Le Touquet. It was a golden time.

But happiness was not made to last. This was something I learned the hard way. When you reach the spot where all the stars align, it can be only for a short time. Fortunately, the memories will be so strong and so bright that they will be able to warm your heart during the many storms to come. And what comforts me is that I was aware of each of my stolen seconds of happiness, and I lived them in full consciousness. Later in my life, I had the chance to live extraordinary moments that I couldn't appreciate entirely for what they truly were. The fantastic memories, of course, remain forever, no matter what, and I cherish each of them deeply, but they are different than what I had those months with Doudou. The truth is that over time, we become more and more greedy, more and more hard to please, constantly pushing higher the pole that holds that sacred "happiness" we all climb after every single day. This is how we forget to live in the moment, by always running toward a vague tomorrow that seems perhaps bigger and more promising than today. The famous French poet Jacques Prévert explained this whole philosophical human problem in one single sentence: "You recognize happiness by the noise it makes when it leaves." I came to understand this later when, caught up in the whirlwind of life, and in a permanent state of desire to go higher, further, stronger, and being terribly afraid of stagnating and failing to live up to the expectations others placed on me, I sometimes forgot to dwell on the beauty of "right now." Luckily, some very hard times made me realize a lot of things and brought me back to the importance of enjoying each and every little thing. Happiness is a butterfly landing on

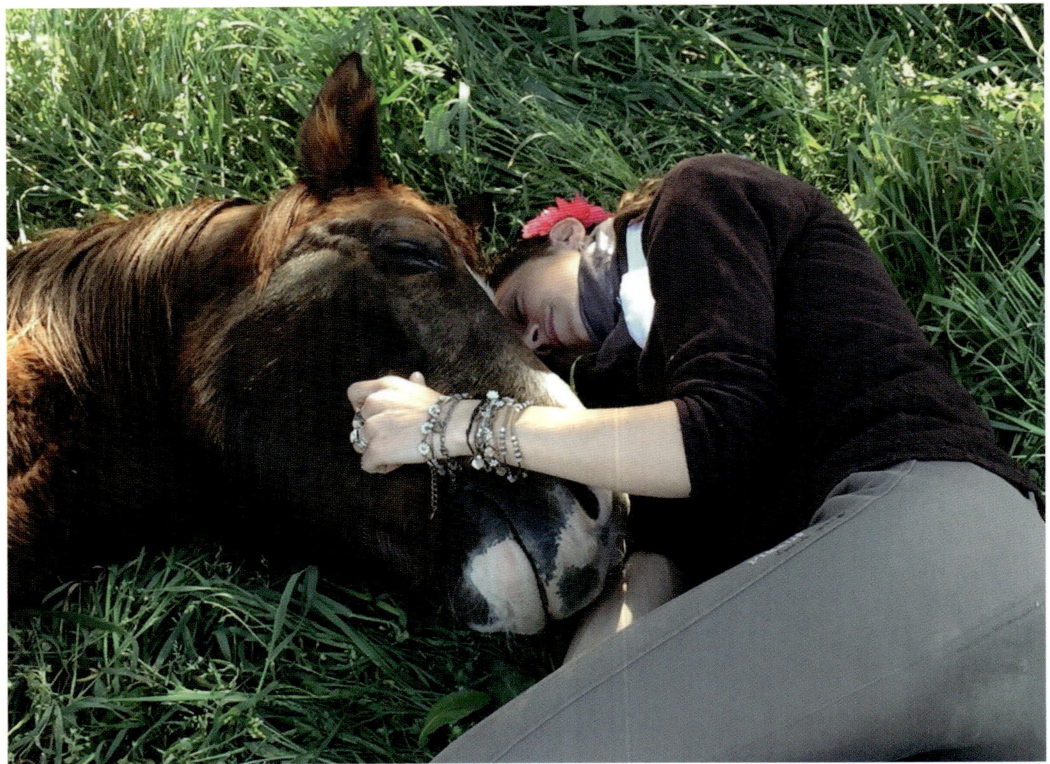

your arm and staying there for a couple of seconds. Knowing this is the only way to bring magic into your life. You need to believe in it first. And sometimes, as an adult, you forget, and you close the door behind you.

After our first international competition, we made our surprise entry on the long list for the European Young Riders Championships. And then the French Championships were to take place ten days later. At the time, I had not thought at all about competing in the European Championships; I was concentrating only on the happiness I was experiencing with Doudou. The news, therefore, came as an additional gift as it reawakened old dreams.

On the last Saturday of June, at the end of my working day, when the Cadre Noir was completely empty, I took my wonderful horse for a hack. We galloped along the marvelous tracks of the National Riding School. The weather was lovely, the sun was setting, the birds were singing around us, and it was just the two of us, alone in the world. Life was good.

Suddenly, in a matter of a few minutes, Doudou was covered in sweat, and then his entire body began to shake. Fabien had told me about these health episodes. He had warned me that it could happen. I immediately jumped down from the saddle and led Doudou back to the stable, simultaneously calling Fabien, who arrived half an hour later. We bathed Donatello again and again. We gave him electrolytes. But his muscles were having spasms that wouldn't stop. My giant became a shadow of himself—fragile and tired. My tears flowed as I ran cold water over his burning body. Tears of fear, of sadness, of guilt. Since then, I have replayed our ride that day in my head, hundreds of times. What if we had finished our ride sooner? What if I had done a light school in the arena that day instead of going out on the trail? According to the veterinarians that day, there was not much that could have been done to prevent what happened. Donatello had already experienced the same kind of symptoms 14 times before. His body was betraying him.

We were at the very beginning of summer 2006 and I had to leave for a two-month internship. Doudou remained in Saumur. I called Jimmy every day to check on the horse I loved. When I returned at the end of August, we resumed light training with him and step by step started to go back at work on a very low-intensity level. Just being back in the arena again, the three of us, felt like a big victory.

Sadly, a month later, Doudou started to have strange new symptoms. One day he was good, the next he was completely lame, then he felt good again. It took weeks of tests for the vet to discover that he was suffering from a form of hoof deterioration.

With his health issues and an injury of my own that I had sustained in December, I didn't ride him for months, but every morning I started my day with him, and every evening, once the stable was empty, I took him for a walk and let him graze. It was my favorite moment of the day. The one I waited for. Being with him was enough for me. One day, however, Doudou's condition suddenly deteriorated. Without our work together, he was not able to move enough, and the lack of motion had triggered laminitis. It was officially the end of his dressage career. The hopes that we might resume our journey in international competition together vanished. What mattered to me now was to offer Donatello a good retirement, because I was convinced that he was crying out his sadness at being locked up in this place that was everything but the one for him.

A few days later, when I came to brush Doudou and spend time with him like I did every evening, I was surprised to find Jimmy sitting in front of Doudou's stall, smoking his cigarette. He should have gone home an hour before. I immediately knew something was wrong. He had red eyes, and when I approached, he said flatly, "They decided to kill him. They say that he won't make it."

As I write these lines, 16 years later, tears still well up in my eyes, and I feel a familiar rage in my throat. I replied to Jimmy that it was not possible. That Fabien would never let that happen. Jimmy answered that Fabien knew about the decision and had not objected. I picked up my phone, called Fabien, and screamed like I've never done in my life. My respect for this man was immense. I adored him as a teacher, as a rider, and as a human being. He was a man dear to my heart. But at that precise moment, the bond that we had woven around Donatello was cut forever. He answered me weakly that nothing more could be done for the horse, that his career was over, that his health would not last. I felt only fury that knew no bounds. I was crying, I was shaking, I was cold—my teeth chattering frantically without me being able to control them. It was the first big shock of my life. I had been told that I was going to lose the one being who had become my whole world, and it was not something I could accept.

The next day, I asked for an appointment with the man in charge of the Cadre Noir's horses and asked to buy Donatello back from the State, whose property he was. The man laughed in my face. He told me that, given I had no money already, it was ridiculous to go and spend the little I had on a horse that would need to be put down three months later. I remained very calm. My decision was made. Donatello would end his life in the South, in the meadow, alongside Bengal, Shapati, Kazan, and the others dear to me. My parents had given their consent. Fabien sided with me.

I wrote a check for 311 euros (or 367—I can't remember which). That was the price of Donatello's freedom and life. He was 16 years old. My father crossed France in one direction to pick us up, and we left in the other, with a giant that was flying away for the first day of his second life.

Doudou spent 11 wonderful and happy years in the South of France. I finished in Saumur in summer 2008 and moved back home, reuniting with my family, my ponies, and the gentle giant who had become more than a king for his new kingdom. He was respected by all—including Kazan! Donatello was the only one in front of whom Kazan bowed, and I don't believe that was because of his size.

As soon as Doudou set foot in his new home, something changed in him. An indescribable peace emanated from his entire being and affected anyone who approached him. He was feeling good and in great shape, so I rode him a few times, just so we could play together a bit more. I don't know which of us had the most fun in those moments. Donatello radiated serenity and happiness, reigning over the kingdom he had made his own.

One moment he gave me ranks above all others. He must have already been 24 or 25 years old at that time and was living freely in the yard. Doudou loved being able to go around, from pasture to pasture, and see everyone. That spring day, he had lain down in the grass, which was a sparkling green, a rarity for that part of France, resting in the shade. I approached slowly and lay down against him. I thought he would move, get up, or push me, but instead he nestled his nose against my neck, and after a few minutes, his hind legs began to move in a cantering motion and his nostrils neighed gently against my skin. Donatello dreamed in my arms. If my life as a rider has given me many emotional moments, this is one of the greatest and most beautiful I had. I wish it never ended.

Donatello died in 2018. He was 27 years old. I think I can say that while he was with us on earth, he was a being of light and wisdom. What he embodied and exuded prompted respect and admiration. As it is still painful for me to write about the end of his life, I will simply share here the text I wrote when he left us:

> **"**

Aged 27, Doudou went to join the stars, under a rainbow formed by the soft sun that shone on the stable at the end of the winter day, and the rain that fell from the eyes of those who loved him so much and who accompanied him on his last journey. He closed his eyes peacefully, after having made a last tour of the meadows and his companions. Donatello was indescribable. He is the horse who, with Mistral, will have most marked my path and my existence. I may have only ridden him for six months, but our lives were linked by something else, which had nothing to do with competition—something bigger, deeper, more real. Doudou was a character, a presence. He was, above all, a free spirit. A unique personality. An identity so strong that it appealed even to those who knew nothing about horses and people just passing by.

The first image of him that I will treasure in a corner of my heart is not that of the incredible colossus who made me dream so much of the dressage and performance arenas, with his extraordinary physicality and the power that made the ground shake under his feet… No, the first image of him that I want to keep in my memory box is the intense serenity that has emanated from him in recent years, and which could be read in his eyes.

Despite his legs, which wobbled a little at times, and his feet, which had altered from disease, little by little, without us being able to do anything about it, a deep peace radiated from him. I don't think I've ever seen or felt this before, in any living being, human or animal. The aura that surrounded him, at the end of his life, was glowing. He commanded respect and inspired plenitude. In 11 years spent in the

At home, I rode Doudou a few times just
for fun—it brought out the best in both of us.

South of France, in our small stable that had become his kingdom, the Grim Reaper came looking for him three times. Three times, however, like an invincible miracle, Doudou chose not to follow and to continue his journey on earth, rediscovering an even greater breath of life than the previous one, as if to affirm that his time had not come, that death should bow down to him. That's why, even if during my last visit I spent a few days to the fullest with him before telling him with a heavy heart that we might not see each other again in this life, the little girl inside me wanted to believe he was immortal. Secretly, I hoped to find him in the same place each time I returned, walking his great body gently, slowly toward me, and welcoming me with that particular raspy whinny of his.

I cannot thank my parents enough for taking such a good care of Doudou over the years, loving him unconditionally, as much as I did. Thank you, and Morgan, for taking the time to make the last three days of his life a true heaven on earth. Thank you for having accompanied him to his final resting place and for having helped him leave with dignity, without suffering, surrounded by the unconditional love that you had for him. I know that from up there, he thanks you at least as much as he did every time he saw you coming, his ears tirelessly pointed forward and his nostrils still quivering. If gratitude had to wear a face, I think it would be his, as it emanated from him every day when any of us came to spend time with him.

Despite the thousands of miles that separated us, when he died yesterday, my heart knew it. My parents, wishing to spare me the difficult decision, did not tell me. Yet, a small alarm suddenly went off in my body, and I felt the immediate need to know expressly how Doudou was doing. When I called my mother late yesterday afternoon, as I have done hundreds of times for no particular reason before, I cannot explain how or why, but I knew deep in my heart that his eyes had closed for the last time. Indeed, she told me hours later, with tears in her voice, that Donatello had taken his last breath at the very moment I called, taking a part of me with him.

The soul of the Froment stable is gone. Donatello du Rivau ENE HN Froment, known as "Doudou," has passed away. Forgive me for not having been by your side, my dear best friend, but I am not sure I would have had the strength to let you go.

In my eyes, you were not only unique, you were invincible.

Joeris made me a dressage rider.

Joeris

The one who showed me that for a horse to open up, you must do so first

Due to Donatello's health issues, I was out of proper training for a period of time. I still rode 8 to 10 horses a day from the school and the écuyers' own strings (they asked for my help because they didn't have enough time for all the horses they had in training), but I was a bit lost with a heavy heart, not knowing what tomorrow would bring. It was a tough period.

One day, having watched me struggle after losing Donatello, Philippe Limousin, the same impressive man who convinced me to leave the theater behind in order to become a dressage rider—twice!—decided to offer me the ride on his own Grand Prix horse, a very special black stallion named Joeris. I had ridden Joeris several times on the trail when Philippe was not there or too overbooked to work his horse, but I had never ridden the stallion in the arena.

I was extremely impressed by that black beauty; you had to respect so many rules around him in order to keep everyone involved safe, as he could choose to be aggressive at the drop of a hat. He, like Donatello, had a special aura. A very special one. He was far from sensational when it came to his movement. His trot was average and the rhythm of his walk very weak—although his canter was beautiful. But, whatever the gait, he exuded such confidence and a presence so strong that you couldn't help but admire him, respect him, and maybe even fear him.

And so there I was, ready to work again, ready to give my everything to live up to the amazing opportunity and the honor that Philippe was offering me. Shoulder-in, half-pass, flying changes, pirouettes, piaffe, passage, so many movements of which I had almost forgotten the flavor, the sensation, the smell…I got off Joeris with pain in my legs and abs, but my head full of dreams again.

Building, moving forward, working, stumbling, stepping back, standing still…and starting all over again. A rider's life is about that—mine is, anyway. In December 2006, there was a clinic for the French Young Riders Team at Saumur with Hartwig Burfeind, a German champion rider and trainer. Philippe offered me the opportunity to ride Joeris in the clinic. I had only worked the horse truly in the movements once at that point— the rest of our rides had only been simple gymnasticization, alone when Philippe was not there, in a snaffle, without any particular goal. But now here I was, in the indoor arena with the *Pôle France* (French team), on this big black stallion that I barely knew, ready to work. I saw some surprised faces, others concerned, and I understood both. I had no right to disappoint them. Then the session began, and Joeris and I were asked to optimize work that we had never done together before: "Pay attention to the regularity of the walk…" "He has to focus on you…" "More seat…" "There is not enough flexion to the left…" I discovered the horse I was riding at the same time as the trainer who was teaching us, seeking a very fast track to harmony and immediate performance.

Then we had to present the Prix St. Georges test at the end of the lesson, which we somehow managed with only a few mistakes, and for a pair who had known very little about each other an hour before, the result was rather encouraging. Philippe looked happy.

The next day, the training session was even better, as Joeris and I started to understand each other. The black beauty still impressed me, but not in the same way, and I felt that he was slowly offering me his trust. I began to experience a sharp pain in my legs from the effort of riding him, but afraid to lose the chance I had been given, I continued, hanging on all week through the clinic, despite the increasingly violent pain, until it became no longer bearable. Upon examination, the doctor's verdict felt like cruel punishment: my adductor muscles on my inner thighs were torn in both legs, which meant a complete stop to all riding, months of rehabilitation, and the end of my story with Joeris before it even began. At least that's what I thought. From the perspective of my 19 years, the sky fell on me. I didn't understand why everything was going so badly. My heart was so heavy, having watched my Donatello for weeks, sinking into his pain. Joeris had given me a little courage, a little strength, but now fate had struck a second time. I thought the world was unfair. I wasn't asking for much, and I was ready to give it my all, to fight, to work hard—and this time, it was my body giving way. Looking back, I know that all of this had a purpose, a reason for happening. I know it built me into who I would become. It was part of the path I had to take to grow, think, and seek.

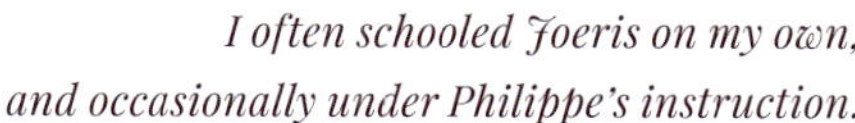

I often schooled Joeris on my own, and occasionally under Philippe's instruction.

But we usually understand those kinds of things only once the storm has passed.

I thought I had missed my chance. Because riding is also—especially when you don't have the financial means to have your own horse—an eternally uncertain future that threatens to collapse at the slightest misstep. But that's how you learn to get back on your feet, start again from scratch, and fight for your dreams. A philosophy that has a name: the school of perseverance.

I was wrong that it was over with Joeris, though. Philippe had decided that I would compete that season with his horse, as soon as I could be back in the tack. So, although still injured, each time the "Big Boss" was away, I started to take care of Joeris as I had done with Donatello—going for a walk in the late evenings, hand-grazing him, longeing him. Little by little, although I belonged entirely to Doudou, the black stallion forced his way into my heart.

Joeris—arrogant, insolent, "bad boy," tough, lonely, sometimes even aggressive and violent—taught me that like humans, you always have to try to understand your horse's personality and scrape off the surface layer before pretending to "get" him. He, who, at first glance, inspired me with more distrust than confidence, and with whom I thought I could only have a superficial relationship due to the rudeness and hardness of his temper, proved to me that individual beings, especially the strongest ones, very often do not show their "true selves" to the outside world. The surface personality is very often the only face that most people want to see. But beneath that, inside, when I decided to really get to know Joeris, a whole different horse lurked in the shadows. Philippe loved him as his own child. You should have seen the way he spoke about his black beauty. Even as a 60-year-old, much-respected Cadre Noir squire, and coach of the French Junior and Young Riders Dressage Team, he became a child again as soon as he pronounced his horse's name. He trusted Joeris so much that he sometimes let him behave dangerously. I can say that he absolutely let the black horse do everything, like a spoiled child. Except that this spoiled child was 17.1 hands tall and weighed some 1,100 pounds of muscle, so his anger and his whims could be very impressive, leading to a complicated daily management of his temper for the other people and animals in his life. That's how everyone—grooms, riders, others in the stables—had started to fear Joeris, and Joeris only built himself up more around that fear. He transformed his own fear into malice, his own timidity into arrogance, and his own fragility into violence. In reality, when you found a way to peek under the shell, when he granted you the privilege of viewing his true self for a stolen moment, you then discovered an incredibly touching and endearing stallion.

Somehow, we made it to the competition season together. I got back in the saddle when I wasn't quite recovered yet, but Philippe told me it was now or never. (I've had relapses of pain ever since that will never go away, but I have learned to live with it. It is another thing that pushed me to think outside the box later on—but that's not part of this story.) I had only been back in the saddle for seven days when Joeris and I made our first appearance in a show ring together. I had to reacquaint myself with him, I had to not let myself be overwhelmed even if I was, and I had to earn his trust and respect by imposing myself on him gently but firmly. There was no question of being fragile in front of Joeris.

We had ups and downs. There was a competition in Spain where we oscillated between third and fourth place in each test. At another, at home in Saumur, the black stallion, on his territory, chose to reaffirm his leadership to the whole world on the first day, but allowed me to climb the slope the next day and succeed in integrating the final test with the music in the Freestyle on Sunday. Each test was different. Each competition taught me a little more about him and about myself. We were moving forward. We were building. One step after another.

Since I had first entered the dressage world two years earlier, 2007 was my first real dressage season. It marked a new turn in my career as I could really learn the ins and outs of riding in the international ring, and I definitely entered the deep end. In June, Joeris and I were one of the six combinations selected for the European Championships, but only four would leave for Switzerland a month later. I was confident, as we had the third best overall results from the whole season, so we would normally be "in." But Philippe called me one day to tell me that despite the good results and the major progress made over the previous months, he could not bring us to the European Championships as it was a conflict of interest with him as the coach.

Suddenly, that was the end of the dream.

Philippe told me that we had to keep training as we were "First Reserve"—in case one of the other combinations had to pull out, we had to be ready and fit to go. At first, I didn't get it. I couldn't. Why did he make me come back to training when I was not yet completely healed, dangling the European Championships before me, if it was clear from the start that Joeris and I could not be selected? Why did he let me hope and fight for a dream that was not accessible? After the incomprehension came disappointment, then anger, then sadness.

I had just fought to save Donatello's life. That was my consolation during this time. Soon I would take him down to my beloved South of France and my family.

Joeris and I still had the French championships 10 days later. At that age I was sometimes overwhelmed by my emotions, and I was highly sensitive and my feelings were hurt, so I initially refused to go. I continued to take care of the beautiful black stallion, but I refused to discuss competition. I was angry, sad, and disappointed, and I felt betrayed. Today I know that Philippe dreamed of the European Championships just as I did, and he thought the three of us could achieve the goal together. Unfortunately, he hadn't foreseen the last-minute pressure he would be under in terms of choosing the team. And I know now that he was sorry and upset about the situation. But when we are young, sometimes we look at the world through a black and white prism, where shades of gray are missing.

However, this disappointment freed me in a way in my relationship with Joeris. I felt freer to explore, try new things, seek new paths and new horizons. We were playing much more together, and it suited us as partners quite well. Philippe obviously taught me a lot, but he was also mostly absent or overwhelmed by his other duties. So, it was mostly by trying, searching, failing, again and again, in front of the mirrors of the imposing indoor arena at Saumur, that Joeris gave me many answers to my endless questions. We were starting to become a real team.

Philippe, who understood how disappointed I was, let me ruminate in my corner and console myself with his horse. But he always kept an eye on us, even from afar. One evening, he called me and said, "It would be a shame not to go to the French Championships when there is a medal to fight for."

He was right.

A little overwhelmed by my emotions, which I struggled to tame at the time (and I still do), our first test at the Championships didn't go as well as it could have, and we ended fourth in the

Each competition was a chance for Joeris
and I to know each other a little bit better.

class. The second day, I was fully back, ready to give my best to Joeris, and we did a good job, ending once again in fourth place. On the eve of the final, the podium was within reach, but it required a faultless Freestyle to move in front of the pair occupying third place at the time.

Musical notes started to play in the air, and Joeris and I had fun like we've never had before in a dressage ring. It was raining heavily that day, the footing was flooded, but we were dancing together, and we were having a blast. When we left the arena, I realized that it had been the first time I had really enjoyed riding a dressage test. Joeris had given me that assurance and attitude that finally released me from all the "rules" and allowed me to be myself again. He and I made our way back to the barn and spent some time together in his stall, quietly, just the two of us. I forgot completely about the competition results, I was just so happy with the beautiful moment we had just shared.

Then Philippe came running to say that the bronze medal was ours.

It often seems that it is when we decide to "let go" that life finally gives us the reward we have been waiting for. It was about my third year involved in the dressage world, and I had always felt I was the foreigner, the outsider, the jumper rider who had arrived there by accident and who still looked out of place. I was not part of the "family." On that day at the French Championships, where I had regained a certain freedom and allowed myself to be myself again, instead of desperately trying to stick to some perceived set of expectations, Joeris made me "legitimate" in the dressage arena.

The following year, I rode our black beauty in a few more competitions, but Joeris was to join Philippe's son in Paris, and for me, another story was about to begin. The most beautiful. The one of a lifetime. The one that changes an entire destiny.

The birth of a philosophy that finds
its roots in the magic of childhood sensations
and feelings, but has evolved through
an endless quest for discoveries and the many
life lessons encountered along the way.

act IV

my personal legends

With Mistral.

While writing these lines, I don't know yet where my fingers will take me in trying to tell you of this journey. Looking back on my childhood and years as a teenager was easy and mostly joyful; I already know that Act IV won't be the same journey. Not because the memories are not beautiful—there are, in this period of time, the most incredible moments that I have yet been given to live. But because these moments are so personal to me, I realize that it is not so easy to talk about them and share them, when each memory is still recent, warm, alive, vibrant.

I have let my typing hands guide me and hope that I was able to keep a clear thread between the different stories in this section. They have intertwined, and in some cases, are still continuing today, as part of an endless evolution. This period of my life marks a decisive turning point, because it is here that my journey truly begins *in full consciousness*. Consciousness of the extent of the path to be traveled, and awareness of how much there is to understand and learn from horses. It is here that, little by little, my philosophy of life with horses started to be forged. This change began with my forever one and only...the most incredible soul I've been given the chance to know: Mistral.

I have to be honest here: Mistral and Sultan, who you will meet next, each deserve an entire book of their own as they have taught me so much about horses, about life in general, and even more about myself. They are my yin and my yang. The father and the son. The white and the black. And as radically different from each other in every way as is the color of their coats.

I owe them everything, and if Mistral has often stolen the show from his son, Sultan—in my heart, first and foremost—today they both form my balance. One does not go without the other in my story. They are complementary. They are exceptional, each in their own way. Two extraordinary beings. Whole. Uncompromising. Extraordinarily sensitive and smart. They are both part of me. Without them, I am incomplete.

I won't lie—it has been difficult for me to recount our 15 years of life together, of ups and downs, of failures and successes, of passion and misunderstanding, in just a few pages. I still don't know how to summarize these two special souls while remaining faithful to who they are and everything they have taught me. However, they are the ones to whom I want to pay tribute most faithfully, because I owe these two horses not only my career, but most of all, the person I have become. They are *the horses who made me*.

With Mistral.

Mistral

My other half,
far beyond words

Donatello had taken the route south, and Joeris, the one of Paris. I was back to nowhere. I started studying philosophy via a distance-learning program; while it failed to ensure me a future, it fed my thirst for learning and understanding.

It was in this context that my phone rang one day. It was Evelyne, a friend I had met at the time I was riding Lambrusco. The Haras du Coussoul Lusitano stud farm was looking for riders for some of their horses because their rider was pregnant. Three days later I was there after taking a train through the night to Mouriès in southern France. The farm was only an hour and a half from my home; therefore, my mother joined me so we could see each other for few hours before I headed back to Saumur.

As Catherine and Sauveur Vaisse, owners and breeders of the horse that was to become my reason for living, introduced all their Lusitanos to me, one by one, I was continually distracted by one particular head and nose, extended over the door of the last stall on the left. When we finally got to the horse, my heart picked up its pace. I hadn't experienced such an immediate reaction before. I had a hard time grasping what was happening—for me, in that barn full of beautiful horses, there was only him. However, Mistral, as he was called, was not the big favorite of the house. With his small frame, lack of strength in the hind legs, and shy temper, he was in the shadow of his neighbor Naxos, whose dazzling personality radiated a thousand lights.

The feeling of "instant knowing" that I perceived in the barn aisle was confirmed when I jumped on Mistral's back. I still remember the smile that I couldn't get rid of. My choice was him. Him and no other. Surprised that I would abandon the flamboyant bay Naxos in favor of the comparatively puny stallion, Catherine looked at me suspiciously, while Sauveur was happy to see that I had really fallen in love with their little Mistral. (Over the years, we would go on to build a strong relationship together—the riding arrangement, which was to last only one year, would extend over 10, and only stopped when a move took me to the other side of Europe.)

What I saw as a sign, if one decided to believe in it, was that both this horse and I bore not only the name of a wind, but the name of two contrary winds. A *mistral* is cold. An *alizée* is hot. His is powerful and devastating. Mine is regular and strategic. Two opposites, who attract each other, to complete each other.

It was with a heart filled with love and hope that I unloaded Mistral from the truck that delivered him to the stables of the Cadre Noir, but the reception he received by others there was the opposite. If I already saw him as sublime—strong, haughty, extraordinary—they saw him only as a small Lusitano with neither quality nor a future. The first months were difficult. We faced mockery and acid remarks. I felt really alone. But despite the disdain of so many, the absolute faith that I had in him made me never doubt that he was going to become a very special horse. If I have always doubted myself (and will probably, always), I never doubted him. For me he was the horse that galloped in my dreams as a little girl. He was my perfection.

Today, when I look back at the photos and videos from our earliest days together objectively, I smile as I recall the comments of some who truly cared about me and were probably just trying to help me see him in a mroe objective way. Because, indeed, in 2007, Mistral was not exactly the king that my heart already saw. He would become that, and even more, later.

To be honest, though, I could never have imagined that Mistral would take me as far as he has and that he would allow me to experience so many crazy adventures, each more extraordinary than the last. We grew up together. We built ourselves together. We became who we are now *together*. Mistral is not a horse to me; he became my best friend, my confidant, my rock, my family. He is my world.

That first year we were in the stable of the "Pôle France Espoir" (developing team) at Saumur, and trained by Philippe Limousin, we gradually began to slowly climb the ranks. It was difficult, however, to show the best of what we were able to do at that time. Something was stuck. I had trained my jumping ponies mainly out of instinct, but dressage, with its strict rules, had forced me into

At first, to others, Mistral looked like nothing special. Below you can see the change already from one month of work together (left) to one year (right).

a mold where I had to learn to discover and understand the ideals. For me, at that time, it was still a discipline I did not know well, and I had not yet mastered all the elements and exercises. The great opportunities to ride Lambrusco, Donatello, and Joeris, each of whom had been fantastic schoolmasters, allowed me to absorb all the new sensations I was experiencing and focus on myself to learn the right aids. Mistral was only seven years old and was not yet confirmed in the requirements at the "Young Riders" level at which we were going to compete. The two of us had to learn and grow together. The experience of one of us could not counterbalance the lack of experience in the other. We were in the same place, ready to climb the mountain together, fail together, get up together, make mistakes together, start all over again together, and stand together—always. But my worst enemy has always been self-doubt, each failure creating in me a feeling of incompetence and powerlessness, of not being up to it and not being worth it, and of disappointing the ones who had placed their trust in me.

These flaws have followed me for a long time. While self-doubt still exists in me and is part of my daily life, I have learned to tame it, but only recently. It has been my biggest weakness. Today, my touchstone is to always question myself and seek every day to become a better horsewoman and person than the day before. I have freed myself from the pressure related to societal expectations. It has been a long journey to get here, but it made me reach a new inner peace.

In sharing this, I've skipped a thousand steps. Let me go back to Mistral and our beginning together.

Lambrusco, Donatello, and Joeris had taught me the dressage movements up to the small tour, with some basics of passage and tempi changes, as well. They had also allowed me to learn how to present these movements properly in the competitive arena. But I still had no idea how much I could build or unbuild, improve or destroy the quality of a horse's basic gaits. It was with Mistral that this realization became clear to me, day after day, and in my eyes, thus began my exploration of the most exciting part of this discipline. Not to be satisfied with what I see at first glance when I view the horse in motion in his natural state, but to know how to grasp the tiny glimpses that he will show along the way during his development, during a few stolen strides, and to realize what he *could* become if I understand him, respect him, believe in him, and do the proper fundamental basic work, gymnastic work, and educational work that will lead him to become the best version of himself.

The first to have introduced me to these concepts was 4* dressage judge Alain Francqueville, who, in 2008, told me again and again that if I wanted to go to the next level with Mistral, I had to work on the depth of his canter. It took me a while to figure out what he meant. I remember those long tours of the arena, focusing crazily on the rhythm, of taming it, feeling like a conductor desperately looking for the right tempo, listening to that invisible metronome. Today, to explain this feeling, I call it "big and slow." It's like you want to suspend the horse's stride in the air and in time, while channeling the powerful energy coming from the hind legs, bringing the canter "uphill" instead of just getting quicker.

During this year, we (all the Young Riders) had a very interesting day with a sport psychology coach, which made me start to realize how much the mental component impacted my performance in the ring. It was the first time I truly considered how emotions, feelings, and energy played a big part in our relationships with horses. I would dig into this even further a few years later, thanks to Sultan, but that first coaching session was a revelation that changed many things. I learned to build a "bubble" around Mistral and myself, and this was probably the first step of what led us, over time, to become closer and closer, until we merged into an inseparable entity.

Freed from the pressure of the eyes of other competitors, their parents and coaches, and the general loud atmosphere during competitions, in the shelter of the cocoon I learned to build around us, Mistral and I began to improve our competition scores. Our evolution was not dazzling but had the merit of being very stable. After starting at the bottom, we gradually climbed the ranks over the months to become one of the four best French Young Riders combinations—and were selected to represent our country at the European Championships in Portugal.

After Clyde and Joeris, where each time I thought I had a real chance at the European Championships without ever reaching them, the news was an explosive mix of joy and relief. All the work, all the sacrifices, all the self-denial, all the lonely days at Saumur, very far from my beloved ones, having left behind the theater and artistic world I loved as much as horses, and having made difficult personal decisions to reach a long-time dream—all of it finally made sense.

Our team finished fourth, which remains the best performance of the French team at the European Young Riders Championships, and equal to the previous year's result. Despite this apparent success, I have mixed feelings about the experience because, as had been the case during Mistral's entire dressage career, after a first very fluid and fault-free test, three judges put him at the end of the first third of the rankings, while the other two, including the French judge, relegated him to the bottom without any explanation other than "he lacks the power of other horses." He would prove them wrong later on, but I felt disillusioned and powerless that day, to see my beloved soulmate so demeaned. He was the youngest horse of the Championships that year, and while it is true that he was not yet the ballet dancer he would eventually become later, he already put his whole heart into giving his very best.

During the individual test, I was distracted by the previous results and less motivated, so we had a couple of mistakes, entirely due to my lack of concentration—but we still managed to get a better score than the day before. Dressage sometimes has its own rules.

A week after we returned from Portugal, Mistral and I took our first steps on stage together, in Tarbes, France, during the outdoor horse fair called "Equestria." I had no idea of the feeling that I was going to discover there—a feeling of being "home," in our rightful place. A new big chapter of our story began with an unexpected encounter with Fabien Galle, then in charge of the Equestria show's programming. Life often has its own plans that we may not be able to see in the moment, yet, when we look back, we understand how much every single experience lived and person met on our journey—good or bad, beautiful or terrifying, successful or unsuccessful—had its *raison d'être*. It's like a giant puzzle with pieces you discover as you are building it.

When I arrived in the damp summer of Tarbes, I discovered the joy of creating with my Mistral, liberated from all shackles, from any pre-established rule. It was an eye-opener. I had never had so much fun with my best friend in competition. Free to be simply us, we found ourselves playing joyfully with the two tempis with which we normally struggled, in the middle of 10 dancers, pirouetting around, and improvised our first strides of passage, encouraged by the spotlights. We had three evening shows in front of 3,500 people, and when the curtain fell behind us on the last one, my heart tightened. It was the first time that the instincts of my childhood crossed paths with the studious rider I had become upon entering the dressage world. This amalgam defines me very well and gives me no real place anywhere. For the dressage riders, I will always be the one they call the "artist," while in the equestrian show world, I will always be the "dressage rider." But it was also this amalgam that forged my destiny with Mistral.

At the end of summer, Mistral and I returned to Saumur and competed in the French Young Riders Championships, where we ended with the bronze medal. Our favorite moment? No doubt it was the Freestyle, which brought us back, for a few minutes, to memories of our summer equestrian shows.

The contract I had signed with Catherine and Sauveur Vaisse, the owners of this extraordinary horse who I knew was my soulmate, ended at that time. As the deadline approached, my heart tightened. I didn't see a future anymore, if it had to be without Mistral. It was only when my phone rang and Catherine offered for me to not only continue my collaboration with my favorite stallion, but to take on a second horse whose current rider was retiring, that I began to breathe normally again. This is how Germanicus, affectionately called "Occus Pocus" at the barn, came into our lives—to the great displeasure of Mistral, who, shy and introverted a year earlier, began to show a new facet of his personality, which was quite possessive and exclusive.

Unfortunately, I can't possibly tell about all the horses who have marked my way somehow, but I will try to pay only a very short tribute to the gray stallion who was not exactly a classic beauty, but who had a heart bigger than himself. Occus Pocus enabled me to take my first steps at the "Under 25" level before trying a 3* Grand Prix that summer. Without him, it would have been much harder for me to bring Mistral to that level. He helped me understand the mechanics and become familiar with the aid sequences. Neither his looks nor his movement inspired me, but the more I got to know him, the more I became attached to the gray—to the great consternation of Mistral, because I can tell you the two hated each other. But my dark-coated favorite had no reason to worry; no other could or would ever dislodge him from his place as "king of my heart." He was my one and only, from the first day we met, and he will remain so, until my last breath.

If there was one particular thing that Occus Pocus made me realize, it was how much tempi changes are a very personal thing. Each rider has his own way of handling them, but we also have to adapt to each horse's sensitivity. For some, the movement will be transmitted without the rider moving his legs at all—just some quick microvibrations at the girth. For others, it will require big movements of the rider's legs, but without touching the horse's belly at all. The "code" might also change along the way as the horse is developing, gaining strength and confidence in the movement. That last key was a very important one, and I owe it to Occus Pocus.

The gray stallion's health was not good as he suffered from arthrosis, which made collected work difficult, and he was retired after a year with me. He still spends happy days at the Coussoul

stud farm where he was born and where he spends his time eating the world famous *foin de Crau* (natural grasses and hay known for its nutritional value) growing in his meadow.

After our bronze medal, Mistral and I left Saumur to return to my beloved South of France where Mistral and I were both born, and to settle in the small family stable where Bengal, Kazan, Shapati, and Donatello were waiting for us. My home sweet home, pieced together by my family over time, had uneven arena footing and small stalls built for ponies, but there, every horse I have known has always been the happiest in the world. I truly believe there is an air of paradise for horses in this place. No frills, no glitter, but a deep serenity.

At the beginning of 2009, we were back on stage because Fabien Galle brought us to be part of the famous *Gala des Crinières d'Or.* I again experienced the same absolute happiness. *But above all...* above all, I met someone who would change everything in my journey with Mistral. French dressage rider Hubert Perring, head of dressage for the Republican Guard (part of the French National *Gendarmerie*, responsible for special security duties in Paris and for providing guards of honor at official ceremonies), was just back from the Beijing Olympics. Because I braided his horse for the show each night, he offered me his help during our last warm-up. The understanding between us was immediate and obvious, and it was the beginning of a collaboration that still continues today whenever our schedules allow it.

Hubert believed in me, and he helped us over the years, every time he could, during competitions or clinics. He used to say that he would not have bet on Mistral at first, but that he was very proud of the incredible horse he became.

It was Hubert who introduced me to an idea that would change everything in my vision of what dressage is. He was the turning point that would mark the true beginning of my own equestrian philosophy. He put his finger on *the* thing that made sense for me. If there is, of course, a common horsemanship education for all, it must be recognized that each horse is different, not only physically, but also mentally. I imagine your inner voice is now saying, "Yes, well, we *know* that already." But it is way more complicated than it sounds. Indeed, if we want our beloved friends and partners to become the best version of themselves, then it is essential we take these two aspects into account, not in a superficial way, as we all already do, but in the deepest sense of the terms. We must give it real attention, a true importance. It takes time to learn to truly discover a horse—to understand who he is, how he works; to know his needs, whether physical or mental; to anticipate his reactions; to reassure his worries; and to calm his excesses. If it takes years to genuinely know another person in her entire self, taking into consideration her past, education, and life journey, then it follows that the exercise becomes even more difficult when you are trying to know an animal who does not speak our language. It is at this point that we fail along the way, all of us. It is here that we make mistakes, all of us. We have the right to make mistakes, as long as we learn from them and use them to grow. Horses have a generosity of heart that leads them to forgive us, as long as our mistakes are made with honesty. What horses rarely forgive are betrayals, whatever they may be.

There is a big difference between "knowing that each horse is unique," and intellectualizing the true sense of the phrase and how it applies in our daily life by the horse's side. To be honest, it requires giving a lot more of yourself and investing yourself very differently than what most riders are prepared to do. As with any couple, the foundation of a strong relationship is based on mutual trust and respect. But in our actual society, in this world where everything is a race and has to be done faster, quicker, and higher, the time needed to truly build that part of the relationship with the horse is not usually granted to us. To get it, to make the time, requires a real inner decision on our part, because the result, for us, will also be a significant inner journey.

I also owe to Hubert how I use my gymnastic and stretching work. It's not about a system. It's about a way of thinking. It's not about doing the same movement from the test 10 times in a row, hoping that it will get better. It's about doing 10 small preparation exercises, working on a very strong and stable base, so when I ask once for the final movement, the horse is able to do it the right way because his body and mindset have been prepared physically and mentally for a few seconds of effort and is ready for it.

The funny thing about Mistral's journey is that, at the beginning, many said we would never get anywhere. After the European Championships, they said we could never make it to the Big Tour. When we made our debut there in 2010, they said it was a feat to have come as far as we had, but we would never exceed 63 percent. And when we started to appear at the prize-giving ceremonies for the national and international Grand Prix, they became silent.

However, Mistral and I have always had a very big flaw that, unfortunately, cost us dearly: the piaffe. Mistral was the first horse to whom I taught the movement, and I had not yet grasped all the mechanics of it. If this was by far the greatest strength of my Occus

Pocus, who helped me discover the fantastic sensation of riding piaffe, it was not that of my soulmate, who, while very elastic, had little strength, and had a lot of trouble understanding the movement. I remain convinced that he could have done it well, if we had started it earlier, and if we had done it from the ground first and not directly under saddle. But I learned the way to teach piaffe as I went along. Unfortunately, he was my "rough draft," my first attempt, the one who allowed me to find the way by failing and starting all over again until it worked.

As the piaffe remained our weakness, and since Mistral got tense as soon as he did not understand something (he always wanted to give the very best of himself), I did not insist, putting the problem aside, relegating it to the background. I loved him way too much to regularly put him under stress just to gain some points during competition. I decided instead to focus on his strengths and work on improving them even more. As time went on, the little stallion with average gaits had turned into a ballet dancer, demonstrating an impressive freedom in his shoulders that gave him a very beautiful feline feel. This is what has always made him special, this is his singularity—an infinite grace that characterizes him when he starts moving.

This period was not easy for me, because we were criticized for this failure in our program. "A Lusitano who does not piaffe? Impossible!" I heard this many, many times, and yet, over the course of my career, I learned that Mistral was far from the only one. I know we could certainly have found a better way to work on the piaffe if my heartbreaker showed up on my doorstep today, with the knowledge I have now. The fact remains that his second weak point was the rein-back, which is a movement linked to the

piaffe, so something was hard for him in this area. I accepted that he could not excel everywhere; he was enough as he was.

Our struggle with piaffe, however, led us to meet different trainers from several countries, including Juan Matute, Sr (Spanish Olympian); João Pedro Rodrigues (head of the Portuguese School of Equestrian Art); Hans-Heinrich Meyer Zu Strohen (director of the Hoya National Riding School); Carlos Pinto (Portuguese Olympian), and Klaus Krzisch (former chief rider at the Spanish Riding School of Vienna). This led to different approaches to this movement and new ways to try to solve our complicated equation. This process was fascinating and worth it, because with each of these horsemen, Mistral and I uncovered clues and understood new things that would help us grow. Curiosity, with a self-questioning and open mind, is one of the most important qualities a rider must never lose during a journey with a horse.

Later on working with other horses and other teachers, I discovered three more ways to teach the piaffe. That's the incredible thing with dressage: there is no one unique way—the answer is different with each horse and moves and changes during his education and along his evolution. What worked yesterday might not work today, and the answer of today might not be the one of tomorrow. This is why you need to always think outside the box, dig into as many techniques as you can, and keep a permanently open mind…in order to find inside yourself each day's answer.

Even if in the end Mistral and I managed to get a semblance of a correct piaffe—not amazing, but no worse than many horses in the competitive arena today—the judges knew of our long months of searching for it. It was too late; it was written in our skins. It was especially hard when several riders who had criticized

Many critics thought Mistral and I would never succeed at international Grand Prix, but we had many rewarding results as competitors.

Mistral harshly in the past approached his owners, proposing to take his ride, arguing that they could solve the piaffe problem quickly. Fortunately, even if perhaps the temptation was there, Catherine and Sauveur never separated us, and most importantly, they gave us the immense opportunity to let ourselves be who we were. Not many people would have done that. It is something I will never forget and for which I will be eternally grateful.

In 2011, as we worked to improve our Grand Prix exercises, an instinct pushed me one day to ride Mistral with his halter instead of his snaffle bridle. It started with a desire to get a breath of fresh air, to find spontaneity in our daily life that was beginning to be too much of a grind, to get out of the shackles of rules, and to play. I remember that simple happiness I felt that day, that emotion that far exceeded what I felt in any prize-giving ceremony, so much so that what was just a random attempt to change things up became a part of our regular training. Even if it wasn't on purpose at first, riding in the halter allowed us to clearly improve the quality of our canter work and especially the changes. Before riding bitless, we were making 23 tempi changes across the whole diagonal of a 60- by 20-meter arena. After, the amplitude of my soulmate's strides had increased so much we got down to only 19, from the beginning till the end.

I also started riding Mistral bareback and filmed it, posting it online, without any idea that sharing it would be the beginning of something far bigger than anything I could have imagined.

A couple of months later, Mistral and I were invited to the Global Dressage Forum in Holland by the renowned Bartels family, key figures in the dressage world. I was only 23 years old and completely overwhelmed by what was happening. Suddenly, we—the shy Lusitano and the young French girl—were in front of some of the most respected professionals from around the globe, demonstrating our bitless work.

Note that at this point the halter had become a bitless bridle prototype with larger and flat pieces to make it more comfortable on Mistral's head. It was my first step toward imagining and building some new material, born from research, experiences, needs, and trials. (Since then, I have worked with partners to release two different models of bitless bridle, designed by me and made by them; and I've developed, with others, bareback pads, a treeless saddle, natural creams, tailor-made organic supplements, light therapy, and other things, always with the passion of improving the welfare and comfort of our beloved best friends while respecting their true nature.)

In the Bartels' impressive Dutch indoor arena, I felt very stressed during the first presentation, having to put into words what Mistral and I were instinctively doing and give explanations for why we were doing what we were truly doing only for the two of us. The second day, I felt better and so did Mistral, freed from my emotions, and we enjoyed participating in the presentation a lot. Afterward, we had many interview requests from all kinds of countries in every language, but I didn't really know how to handle it, because the truth was that we were doing what we were doing *only for us*. We weren't doing it for a cause. We weren't doing it to denounce or defend something. We were just doing it for us, because that's simply who we were and where we were on our journey together.

In parallel to our competition schedule, Mistral and I had continued regularly participating in artistic equestrian shows. *Ballerines* was created during the summer of 2011 with my friend Aurélia, who was one of the dancers we'd been working with in Tarbes. A beautiful friendship emerged between the three of us

and still continues today. Mistral and I took our first steps under the spotlights bitless in this show, and we traveled from France to Italy, passing through Germany, to perform this number at many beautiful events, in front of several thousand people, over the next few years.

If Mistral has always been and still is my great love, one thing almost broke us apart. It has been, in our 15 years together, our only real clash. But it was also a turning point in our relationship, as well as in my equestrian philosophy.

The better Mistral became, the more his personality grew—and it grew as much as his talent. In 2012, he turned into a stallion with a very strong temper, claiming his place as head of my entire world to everyone moving in his kingdom without his permission. While he was always focused and brought boundless generosity to our work, he showed a growing impatience in other aspects of our daily life, and most problematically, became extremely possessive toward me, getting more and more aggressive with the other animals I took care of. Alaya, a Miniature Spitz, had been my shadow since my eighteenth birthday. With her little black fox look, she followed me absolutely everywhere. When I had to leave for Saumur five days after turning 18, moving 500 miles from my home sweet home, Alaya had come with me, providing an extension of my family—a little piece of them that I could take along. I loved Alaya as much as Mistral, just in a different way. There was room for both of them in my heart. Unfortunately, they didn't feel the same way. They were always provoking each other, bickering, and giving each other the side-eye. They slowly became enemies.

It was the only time I thought I should leave Alaya home while I traveled to coach my brother at an international jumping competition. She'd had a puppy a few weeks earlier and looked tired, so I thought it would be more comfortable for her to stay.

A thousand times, I have played the mental film of this decision over and over again in my head. A thousand times, I have blamed myself. A thousand times, I have wanted to go back in time.

I remember my phone ringing on our way back from the competition. I remember the panic on the other side of the phone. I remember not understanding anything and talking, trying to be calm and find out what was wrong. And then I heard, "She left us when she heard your voice. She knows that you were by her side." I remember each word, one by one.

Then, I fell into nothingness. First, I refused to understand—the denial to which we cling when faced with the inconceivable. Then, for five days, I couldn't get out of bed, couldn't eat; I ceased to exist. Morgan, my younger brother of 10 years, would crawl in next to me, playing stupid movies on his computer, and trying to gently invite me to come back to life. It was the sweetest idea of a 14-year-old boy, helping his sister in her first real grief, but I remained absent. A part of me was gone. I didn't know how to continue without her. And the hardest for me to process was that the one who took Alaya from me was my other half. I was lost, torn.

One of the important stages of grief is anger. But I couldn't complete that step. I could not hate the one who had caused the pain, but I could no longer love him, for I saw in him the one who had killed my sweet little black fox.

On the sixth day I got up, brushed Mistral, and we went for a long walk together as the sun set. We repeated this for two weeks. I needed to feel him again, to be with him again, and at the same time I did not feel able to re-establish any real dialogue with him. We walked in nature, accompanied by the singing of birds and the sublime light that characterizes the beloved landscapes of my childhood. Little by little, an inner peace started to come back to me.

I waited for a clinic with Hubert to ride Mistral in the arena again. I was afraid of blaming him, being unfair, not managing my emotions if anything went wrong. But, as if he had grasped the importance of the moment, Mistral put even more heart than usual in his work, and step by step, finding him again, finding my feel, I got back on my feet.

It was the first time I realized how jealousy is not just a human trait, but a true element of horse behavior too. I don't believe that I am anthropomorphizing, but I have chosen since that day to try and understand the personalities, behaviors, mistakes, needs, and insecurities of each of my horses by the same criteria I would use for humans. In doing so, I have observed in them behavioral similarities far greater than I previously thought possible. The only true difference, I find, is that horses don't know how to cheat, lie, or manipulate, which therefore makes it easier to know who they really are. Some will say these words are "crazy" or my ideas are too far "out there." I am not claiming that I am right or wrong, only that these are my beliefs and the path I have chosen to follow. I try to understand who each horse is in order to amplify his personality to the maximum and let him express himself, because that's what gives him that extra spark in life.

I am certain that this philosophy is not the easiest path for working with horses, because it encourages them to feel self-confident, strong, and happy to be who they are, which leads to their autonomy and independence. It is no longer a question of a horse who works with you because he has no choice. He becomes a decision-maker too, and this can lead to excesses if it is not properly managed. Many confuse kindness and fairness. If I always want my horses to feel responsible for themselves, they must do so according to the established rules of life. Like raising a child, loving a horse is, before anything else, educating him, giving him limits and guidelines. Too often, I see people in very dangerous situations because they don't understand that limits can be about loving someone. A horse who does whatever he wants, wherever he wants, whenever he wants is like a child without boundaries or guidance: lost.

Horses are born with a gregarious instinct. They need a leader or a mentor to feel safe. If we do not become that person to them, then they will have to fill that role themselves. It is a matter of survival for them. Behave as a leader—fair, straight, confident, frank—and your horse will follow you to the end of the world, for you will become his place of safety.

And although I do make comparisons between human and horse character traits, and I do find many similarities, I also know it is essential not to confuse everything and remember that horses remain animals. Big ones. With their own language. My friend director, actor, and liberty trainer Jean-François Pignon always says something that I find to be so true: "Horses will never learn to speak our language. It is our duty to make that effort. It is up to us to learn to speak theirs." And this is absolutely the hardest thing to do. That's where we who work with horses make the most and biggest mistakes each and every single day. But allowing us to fail while trying is allowing us to learn, and therefore to make progress as well.

In 2013, my world was about to change from one day to another and everything around to fall apart. Without benchmarks anymore, lost, I desperately hung on to Mistral, my pillar in the storm, my anchor, my lighthouse in the night. It was during this eventful period that I rode Mistral for the very first time with a kind of neck rope, which was in fact a lead rope, at this small stable where we were at that time, located at the foot of the famous mountain Sainte Victoire, close to the beautiful city of Aix-en-Provence. It was nothing, just two rounds of trot on a circle and a long hug. Just my inner child knocking at the door.

It would be another year, one with an increasingly difficult daily life, marking my true transition to adulthood and a farewell to naivety, candor, and innocence, before I braided a rope out of baling twine, tied it around Mistral's neck, and jumped on my heartbreaker a second time with nothing more. We were in Belgium, alone early one Sunday morning in the Olympic-sized indoor arena, with our blended breaths as the only soundtrack and Myriam, the same person who filmed us while riding bareback and bitless the first time, again our only witness. What was initially only a deep need for room to breathe, being one with my one and only, finding my roots, gradually became movements of the Grand Prix. After a small warm-up in walk and trot, with an improvised bareback pad that was extremely uncomfortable and slippery but important to protect my champion's spine, I remember trying a few steps of leg yield before starting in canter. Then, across the diagonal with the three tempis, two tempis, tempis, and finally the pirouettes on the sacred center line. At the end, it didn't matter how much my entire world around outside the arena was collapsing. I had Mistral, and as long as he was there, I would stand, no matter what. He made me strong.

What followed in my life was a series of hard times. I ended exhausted, but I stood up, because of Mistral. The light needs the

shadow to shine. More than ever, I understood that it is in the difficult moments of life that we grow, that we jump to the next level of our journey, transcending ourselves because we have no other choice left, like the phoenix rising from his ashes, stronger than before.

In September of 2014, on our way back to France due to an emergency, I was surprised to be invited to Saumur, where my history with Mistral began, and where he had been so criticized by "the men in black," to demonstrate our work with the neck rope during the heritage days hosted in Le Cadre Noir. As during our presentation at the Global Dressage Forum years prior, it was not easy for me to find the words to explain what I was doing yet, because the moments bridleless and bareback were personal to us. They belonged to the two of us. We were in front of everyone feeling naked, just showing who we were together.

I was not prepared for the acid and crazy attacks that a woman sent me that day, following our demonstration. I didn't understand her rage, her need to smear us, to stomp us. It is only recently that I have realized that the hatred that some send us is in fact only a reflection of their own failures, setbacks, disappointments, scars, limitations, fears, bitterness, and sadness. Although it is always difficult for me to take a step back, as I am an extra-sensitive person, doubting and questioning myself all the time, I now know that it should not be taken personally. The root of this anger comes from elsewhere. We are only the recipient of it. That's the other side of being in the spotlight, whether you want it or not. There is no possible discussion, no constructive exchange that can be had, because whatever you may

My inner child, the one who had found great
freedom and happiness on her ponies, thought
of riding Mistral with nothing but a neck rope.

say will only be heard and perceived through a distorted prism. I have long wanted to fight the injustice I perceive when this kind of incident happens (luckily, very rarely to me, I have to admit), refusing to be saddled with intentions that I never had or to be linked to stories of a past that is not mine or to be given a personality that is not me at all. But going up against these situations is like trying to fight windmills. You hurt yourself and exhaust yourself for nothing. Letting go of it all and knowing who you are deep inside is the only answer.

In January 2015, the equestrian show *Phoenix* debuted—brand new, black and red, on fire. The first show where Mistral and I were alone on stage. Our first show with the neck rope. The first chapter of our second life. We tried it first at an invitation-only meeting in Avignon, reserved for organizers of international horse shows, followed by Verden and Herning. At Equitana in Essen, Germany, and its famous nighttime *Hop Top Show*, I switched my flamboyant outfit for a white princess dress at the request of the show director. *Pure Harmony* was born—and suddenly we were requested everywhere.

Before even realizing what was happening to us, Mistral and I were caught in a whirlwind that would not end for two and a half incredible and marvelous years, going from one performance to another, traveling the whole of Europe, up and down. I had to give up my role training the French Pony Team exactly five years after I had taken it on. It was not the easiest decision to make, but I couldn't be everywhere at once, and for the first time since

I got him, after working like hell and riding dozen of horses for owners without one single day off, break, or holiday for seven years in order to be able to handle Mistral's career's costs, I finally got the chance to focus only on him, his son Sultan, and later on, our little sunshine Pirate (who I will tell you about soon). It was the best gift I'd been given, and it brought us even closer (at least, it brought me closer to each of them, as Mistral, of course, hated both Sultan and Pirate) and helped me realize how much the time spent with and given to our horses is the key to everything.

In June of 2015, the organizers of the CDI4* in Mallorca, Spain, asked me if it would be possible for Mistral and I to both compete and perform an evening show at the event. I agreed, thinking it was a perfect farewell to competition for us: a fantastic place, a shiny atmosphere, the Grand Prix on Friday, a performance of *Pure Harmony* on Saturday evening, and the Freestyle on Sunday. We left the competitive arena for the last time with a seventh place finish and proof that Mistral was a unique horse, able to switch from competition mode to artistic show with disconcerting ease. When I think about him, along with the smile that comes straight to my face and the stars that immediately shine in my eyes, I always have, "What a horse!" coming straight to my mind.

In 2017 we performed in the same arena that had changed our destiny two years before, that of Essen, Germany. That of Equitana. Several months pregnant, I was about to take the road to the Czech Republic, where a new future awaited us. It was our first show as a foursome, and a very special and emotional one for me. Mistral and Sultan, father and son. And me and Louise, mother and daughter—even if Louise was still only in my belly.

There's a pretty amazing story about my pregnancy. In February, during our show in Leipzig, Germany, Mistral was not at all his usual self. He seemed angry. In the arena, during our performance, he was, for the first time, not listening to me at all. I didn't even recognize him.

After several weeks dealing with this unexplainable mood that was so unlike him, my mother suggested I try an animal communicator. To be honest, it wasn't something I believed in, but I was so sad to see my horse as he was, I ended up agreeing to talk to the woman my mother found. Well, after mentioning a few banalities that anyone could have said after reading my social media posts or the press about us, the lady said, "You are sick, and it worries him a lot because you don't know it, and he is terribly afraid of losing you. It's something in your belly, and it's only going to get bigger and bigger."

It had only been a few days earlier that I had discovered I was pregnant. No one else in the world knew about it yet. With tears in my eyes, I told the animal communicator what was going on. She replied that Mistral needed me to explain what was happening and to reassure him.

And so I did—when we were alone, just the two of us—feeling a little bit silly, talking to him with my butt in the shavings of his stall while he was eating his hay, pretending to ignore me.

Believe it or not, from that day on, Mistral became himself again. Some of you will roll your eyes at this story. I understand, as I was like you! But the episode shook me.

And then, 10 years after we first met, Mistral finally became all mine, so we could never ever be separated.

I continued to ride and work Mistral as usual, until exactly 20 days before I gave birth. I was lucky enough to have a very easy pregnancy that allowed us to continue our daily life together. I was just a bit heavier on Mistral's and Sultan's backs. We were adapting to a new daily life, settling down after a long time on the road, and building a brand new universe for us; with so much change, I felt other aspects of our routine should follow course as usual. What I had not anticipated, however, was how the arrival of my daughter would change my life so radically. I was born a second time with her. As the most beautiful gift, she decided to arrive earlier than expected, the day after my thirtieth

birthday. It's hard to imagine a more exceptional present to celebrate entering a new decade.

On the other hand, I was rocked much more than I wanted to acknowledge by this tornado of love that suddenly overturned everything in its path. Before that, Mistral (for ten years), Sultan (for seven years), and Pirate (for two) had been my everything. My whole life was entirely dedicated to them. Every decision I made was based on them, for them. And suddenly, I didn't know how to manage the crisscrossed emotions I was feeling. I wanted to be the best mother for my little girl, but I wanted to remain the same pillar of safe haven to my beloved horses. I struggled a lot, as I never had before, and if I had to be honest, I would admit that I truly and finally found my peace and answers only recently. It took me three years to process and accept that, from that twenty-first of August, 2017, my relationship with the horses in my life would have to be different and that it was not a betrayal. I was deeply lost, trying to fill my absence with more and more people around them, specialty care, and attention. But it was in vain because it did not replace *me* or *my time*. I was consumed by guilt, trying to be everywhere, and ultimately, failing to be anywhere the way I really wanted to be.

Mistral never blamed me. He did not alter in our interactions, but he rejected Louise, refusing to look at her, pinning his ears and hardening the look on his face every time he heard her "chirping" around. We were like this long-term married couple, suddenly jostled by something bigger than us that we didn't know how to handle and overcome. The love and link between us remained intact, but our daily life together changed.

It took me a long time to intellectualize and accept this new reality, especially since other events threw us into the three hardest and most painful years I ever had. Again, as terrible as it was, the dark times allowed me to take an inner journey that was very important on my path to personal growth, finding new understanding, and taking new steps forward. I could make it because of her, my little princess, and because of him, my one and only. We came out the other side together stronger, much more centered, and freer too.

In 2018, it was time for Sultan to take over from his father at the legendary Aachen, Germany, showgrounds. I had imagined for this great return to the stage, our first following the birth of Louise, a special number, with me wearing white feathered wings, measuring 16 feet from one end to the other. It was an idea that had been in my head at the time of creating our show *Phoenix*, but this time, the wings were truly there, incredibly impressive and beautiful. The number was called *Angelus* and was entirely groundwork.

But 10 days before the premiere, a terrible colic took my white angel to the emergency veterinary clinic. When Sultan's general condition was back on track and I was ready to go get him, I received a terrible call, saying that he had caught a bacterial infection, which was attacking his entire nervous system. After three days of waiting, not only did he recover, but he regained all his strength, keeping only a fragile and sensitive stomach that we have monitored very closely every single day, ever since. Of course, it took Sultan long weeks to regain his energy and start rebuilding his body again, slowly, one step at a time. With only five days left before we were to depart for Aachen, I decided to improvise a new show with my heartbreaker. Mistral and I had already presented *Pure Harmony* two years earlier, so we had to do something else.

Mistral's official retirement farewell was scheduled for December in Sweden. I already had in mind that I wanted to try to ride with the wings, a symbol of freedom, for this moment that I obviously wanted to be very special, but it was very complicated because I planned to ride only with the neck rope attached to my waist.

Against general opinion, I decided to try it in Aachen. I trusted Mistral, despite the fact that this new challenge was a potentially very dangerous one—and that we had only five days to make it happen. Everybody on the team was extremely stressed.

The first day I introduced the wings, Mistral crossed the entire arena backward. The second, he accepted touching them, and I could very carefully put them on. The third, we tried a few movements, with the rope in one of my hands and the wings in the other. The fourth, we tried a draft of the choreography, which was even harder than expected because the neck rope, attached to my waist, could not be released as I normally always did. The tension on it was permanent, which created confusion and misunderstandings. I softened the feel of the rope with a thick gel pad to protect his neck, and this was a great step forward, but we were pressed by time.

When we arrived in the German city, Mistral became super tense. The presence of ponies and mares with foals drove him out of his mind in a way they never had before. Despite this concern, the dress rehearsal worked out okay, and we were able to try the full choreography for the very first time. The warm-up for the first evening show, however, was a disaster. In the indoor arena next to ours were all the mares. My stallion no longer responded to anything I asked, and I started to be scared that, for the very first time, he would let me down. Finally…it went fine. There were imperfections, but the audience hadn't seemed to have seen them. As I always bear the weight of my own high expectations on my shoulders, I was a bit disappointed, with the taste of "unfinished task" on my tongue, but the rest of the team, knowing everything we'd overcome, was super proud and relieved.

The second day, everything felt radically different from the first minute on, leading us to the highest point of our entire career. It was an evening that will always remain our evening. Our greatest one, where all the stars perfectly aligned. Without exactly picturing it, I'd been living for that moment since I started riding. I understood that culmination while enjoying an extraordinary feeling. Perfection. That moment when everything around stopped. Where our breaths were in unison. Where we were one. I think it is what being a centaur would feel like. In our long career together, Mistral and I had known several standing ovations, but this one was different. It had another flavor. It was a suspended moment. I couldn't sleep that night because my adrenaline was still so high, my emotions too intense. I couldn't stop smiling, and I had butterflies all around—outside and inside—just reliving it. I realized how lucky I was to live such a moment once and to be able to say, "I know what it feels like, and it is, along with love, the most powerful emotion ever."

Mistral's farewell was in Stockholm as planned, in the arena that had hosted one of our most iconic shows three years before. In a month, he was going to be 19 years old, with five years of international Grand Prix competition behind him, all while performing at artistic equestrian shows, followed by three years on tour around the world. I wanted Mistral to retire before getting tired, while still at his best, happy to go…wanting to go.

I have to thank the whole Sweden International Horse Show team for everything they did, because they organized the evening so the moment would be perfect—and it was. The King and Queen of Sweden were in attendance. The event was broadcast live on a major Swedish national channel. It was an amazing and well-deserved farewell and honor for a little horse that many laughed at before he grew into something magnificent.

But it was hard for me to realize that our journey together was about to take a new turn—the last one. Looking back, remembering all our adventures together, the wonderful people Mistral and I had met on our path, the challenges we overcame, our failures, our hard times, our discoveries, our victories. We had been growing up together, and suddenly, I felt old, because I had to accept that Mistral was starting to be. I grew old with him that day. Half of me did.

With a very heavy heart, I massaged him backstage for what I thought would be the very last time, preparing him for our performance in silence, tears rolling down my cheeks. I was not myself, and of course, he felt it. The world around seemed distant, smothered, in slow motion. I wish I'd had the strength and the courage to enjoy every minute of his special moment, but the truth is that I was totally stunned. The emotion felt by our entire team was immense. Each person had special memories with this legendary horse.

Luckily, that night, Mistral was standing strong for both of us. He seemed to say, "Don't worry, it's gonna be okay." In the last minute backstage, after everybody left us to go into the stands, we were alone for a short, shared breath before we entered the ring for our last dance. When the curtain went up, all the spectators

turned on the light on their phones, projecting a starry night all over the big stadium, moving me to tears and giving me goosebumps that wouldn't leave me during the whole performance, because I remembered, just then, a promise I had made Mistral during one of our very first competitions—in Jardy, in 2008, where we failed.

"One day," I had told him, "your name will shine among the stars."

We took a final lap of honor among all the shining stars. And as the arena door opened for our exit, Mistral and I turned back, and I did what everybody had made me promise not to do with the wings for safety reasons. I untied the rope connecting my waist to his neck, and he and I did what we loved the most. I leaned my shoulders slightly forward. He knew the signal, taking off at full speed, and we crossed the arena one last time, the wings flying in the air. In that gallop, we closed 12 years of history. Our story. The one of a dark brown stallion and a young girl with green eyes, neither of whom were predestined to succeed, and who, together, defied imposed rules to follow their own path toward happiness, leading them to the highest emotions one can feel in a partnership with another being.

Today, after having traveled together in France, Germany, Holland, Belgium, Spain, Italy, Austria, Denmark, Sweden, Portugal, England, Czech Republic, Qatar, and Switzerland, Mistral flows through happy days at our home in Belgium. At nearly 24 years old, he is still stunning and in great shape. It was difficult to find the right balance once his retirement was decided. I think that we found it in the rhythm that we have today, and in which he seems to have blossomed fully. Twice a week we do what I call his "little yoga of the day." These are 20-minute sessions to help maintain his physique so he can age in a body that

In Stockholm, the audience lit up the stadium like a night sky,
and Mistral could shine amongst the stars.

remains comfortable for him. Then we hack in a neck rope once or twice a week. The rest of his time, he spends in the meadow, watching over a kingdom in which no one goes in or out without his consent, or at least his opinion. As I write these words, he is grazing in front of my window. I love sitting in my kitchen and seeing him enjoying his existence. Every day, he gets his massages and daily attention. He needs it. When I go away for a few days, he gets tense and anxious, so sometimes, I call to talk to him, and he always calms down when he hears my voice. We have our rituals. Here, the whole life of the stable is organized around the king. That's not an option for me. He deserves it all. The more he grew during his journey, the more a special aura shone around him. He is one of the world's special souls, I guess. All those who meet him say so.

For the fiftieth anniversary of Equitana, we broke the rules a little bit, and Mistral set foot under the spotlights again. Five years before, we had been performing our first show, the four of us, with Sultan, and with Louise comfortably sitting in my belly. This time, she was sitting on top of Sultan. *Rising Generations* came to life in the arena where we had all our biggest turning points. Father and son. Mother and daughter. United for a last show.

From Belgium, Essen was only three hours away. Everything was organized with the team of the Hop Top Show so that Mistral could appear under the best conditions ever, staying in his home meadow until the very last minute, and enjoying optimal comfort once on site. If you could have seen the happiness that radiated from him as soon as he got off the truck! He exuded joy being back in an atmosphere that he so loved. And above all, a serenity in his eyes. He who usually prowled constantly in his stall, kicking the walls like hell whenever another horse dared to move somewhere else in the barn, was peaceful, quiet, and where he belonged. Three and a half years after seeing the spotlights for the last time, he was back with the exuberance of a six-year-old discovering the world. To see him this way—shining, proud, full of power, playful—was indescribable. It went beyond words.

If Mistral was the blessing of my life, meeting him so early in my journey was my curse. He rocked my world when I was only 20 years old. He gave me everything I could dream of, and much more. Unfortunately, humans travel these roads longer than horses. Finding the successor to a horse so exceptional is an impossible task to fulfill. There will never be a second Mistral. He will always remain the first. The one and only. The king I learned everything from and discovered everything with. I loved every single second of our journey.

It took me a long time to realize how heavy the burden of our connection was for others. It also took me time to understand that, now a mother, I could no longer have another story as passionate, strong, and fusional as the one I had with Mistral, because now a little girl has become my absolute priority. It's not just about me anymore. Now my story comes after hers.

I fought against my feelings for many months, lost in a whirlwind of conflicting emotions without exactly understanding what was truly going on, what was hiding behind these struggles. Today I am at peace, because I was finally able to put words to what tormented me. What I had with Mistral was unique. It was a love story. A real one. He won't have any replacement. He will not have a successor. It can't be, simply because my life will never be the same again. We were everything to each other for almost 15 years. That's what made the whole difference.

I am him and he is me. Together, we are complete.

I am him and he is me.
Together, we are complete.

With Sultan.

Sultan

My biggest master

Sultan is the son of Mistral, born six years after him, as light as his father is dark. Together, as I have mentioned, they are my yin and my yang. Our path hasn't been an easy one, but it has been, without any doubt, the one that made me grow the most. When I tell others how difficult Sultan has been, I see in people's eyes how much they don't believe me, and it makes me smile inside.

Today, Sultan could live in our house with us. He is part of us. Year after year, he gradually assumed a place in my life I would have never been able to imagine, and we owe our powerful and strong relationship to the struggles we had to go through together. Even if it's hard for me to say it out loud, Sultan is, today, closer to me than any other horse, including Mistral, whose special

place in my heart will remain forever. And this is despite the fact that, now that I am a mother, my entire world has changed, so I will never put the same time, dedication, energy, and involvement into any other horse, that I did with Mistral, and to some degree, with Sultan later on.

I started riding Sultan at the Coussoul farm where he and his father were born. He was three years old, dark gray, with dapples. He was tall, where his father was small, with a very strong neck and a light croup, but he was Mistral's son, and for that, I already loved him. I presented him at the stallion grading in the summer, but because of a particular detail in the conformation of his hind legs, he was refused, so Sultan went back in his field for more than a year. I started to work him again during his fifth year in order to prepare him to be sold. He was extremely smart and super sensitive, but his gaits were too limited, so nobody was interested in him.

It was at this time that a woman decided to buy Mistral without ever having seen him, without even knowing him, without having tried him—just like buying a pair of shoes on Amazon. I was destroyed, annihilated, empty. I was going to lose my soulmate. I was going to lose the one that had become my entire world. The future had no meaning anymore, no flavor. Nothing made sense. Mistral did not belong to me; he was going to go more than 600 miles away, leaving me behind with my heart broken in a thousand pieces.

That's when, in an act of survival that I long believed was one of my biggest mistakes, when in reality, everything would make sense later on, I made the choice to buy Sultan. Since I had no money, I got a loan. If the horse of my lifetime was to leave me, then his blood would always flow into a horse that no one could take away from me.

A few days before Mistral's departure for his new home, the
veterinary pre-purchase visit having been accepted and the details
of the sale settled, unexpected news changed everything. The sale
of my heartbreaker was cancelled, and Mistral stayed with me. Life
had reactivated its wheels. Our destiny was in motion.

And then Sultan, the horse I had bought as a form of insurance,
arrived home, to the kingdom of his father, who began by hating
the newcomer who came to shake up our routine and daily life.

To his credit, the tall gray asked for a place by my side, and
the more he did, the more my heart closed down. Mistral was
the only one. Although his blood flowed through the veins of
Sultan, the two had, apart from an extraordinary finesse of mind,
not the slightest commonality. They were the perfect opposites.
Where my beautiful brown stallion was all supple and elastic, the

gray son was quick and short in his movements, "running after"
his legs. My memory had erased the difficult road I had already
traveled with Mistral. Sultan had to grow up in the shadow of
his father.

I brought Sultan into my life because I wanted a part of his
father to be mine forever, but Sultan wasn't up to it. I made him
bear my disappointment, which had nothing to do with him. This
was one of my youthful mistakes. Little by little, Sultan locked
himself in a bubble. He built his own world, in which I was no
longer welcome. We were two strangers with broken hearts, trying
to hold the pieces together. If Mistral was my soulmate, his son
was always my mirror. We were stuck, side by side, unable to go
toward each other. While I always had an indestructible faith in
Mistral's talent, despite everyone's opinion, I was unable to believe

in Sultan. Everything brought me, every single day, to the same conclusion: he would never become his father.

In December of his fifth year, Sultan went to the north of France for a month, at the request of his breeder Catherine, to collect his semen. He had been a peaceful stallion until then, but he returned unmanageable. He was a lion, fighting everything. It was no longer possible to transport him in the same truck with Mistral, as together they would destroy the whole trailer. He hurt himself every single time I took him somewhere. He wanted to be the chief, no matter what. I often feared for his life, as he had no limits. How many times would I have to heal his wounds, fix what he broke? And yet, the strange thing was that I couldn't give up on him. Something bound us together.

At that time, I realized that Sultan wasn't meant for competition, certainly not international sport, which was the main part of my daily life. He, who hated imposed rules, who always needed to know that he had a choice, could not get into that sandbox. He was the first horse to show me that, like humans, we must find the right role for them, if we want to give them the chance to flourish and bloom one day. Not all horses are meant for competition. Not all are meant for shows. Not all are meant for liberty work. Not all are meant for dressage or jumping. The most common mistake made every single day by all of us is to push horses down paths that are not theirs, but the ones we have in mind for them.

Since Sultan, I look at each horse who comes to our farm through a different lens, taking the time to discover who they are at the deepest level first, in order to understand who they are meant to become, and to try to help them get there.

Sultan is a particularly smart horse—even more so than his illustrious father—but it took him five years to understand the flying change. I honestly thought we would never get there, which is hard to imagine now that he is doing a hundred tempis by my side at liberty, without my help. But since then, this movement has honestly remained my stress point with young horses. As soon as it is understood by one of my horses, a weight is lifted from my shoulders, and nothing seems difficult to accomplish anymore. This feeling is always my main focus with the young ones.

I think I can say that, thanks to Sultan, I probably know nearly each and every possible method, way, and exercise to help a horse understand how to do a proper flying change: from the inside to the outside, from the outside to the inside; on the short side, on the long side; on the circle (20 meters, 10 meters); on the quarter line, on the diagonal; in a shoulder-fore, in the travers, in the leg-yield (steep, shallow, counter leg-yield); in the serpentine, from true canter to true canter, or from counter canter to counter canter; with transitions, without transitions; with the neck up, with the neck down; with my seat in the saddle, with my seat raised out of it; with my legs at the girth, a bit behind the girth, or far behind the girth; touching the belly with a short direct cue, a very soft but longer-lasting cue, or just barely brushing it; using the half-halt on the outside rein, on the inside rein; on long reins, short reins, with both in one hand, and both in both hands; with inside flexion, outside flexion, and absolutely no flexion; in a very collected canter, in medium canter; with vocal cues, without vocal cues; using micro-touches with a whip...and not.... I could probably write an entire book about this process alone! For some horses, flying changes are super easy and come quite naturally. In one lesson, the movement is done, understood, settled. For others, it can take years—and be the cause of many (big) headaches.

But once a horse learns them, flying changes are one of my absolute favorite movements. I love that "dancing" feeling so much—and the road that leads to

Sultan and I are often happiest together,
exploring beautiful movements
with only a neck rope.

the tempis is like a puzzle. You put the pieces together, one by one, slowly, playing with tempo, and mainly ensuring they are clean and correct, until one day you get the whole picture. You never know when the moment is going to come, but you do know it will come eventually, and each time I can help a new horse reach it, I get the same magical feeling.

It took me five years to find it with Sultan. Five years to achieve a single correct flying change on each side. I chose to start building toward the movement quite early, the year he turned five, knowing that for Iberian horses, changes can prove to be one of the biggest challenges during the course of their training. I thought the younger we started, the better it would be for Sultan. I remain convinced that, when the quality and the balance of the canter is sufficient, it is good to introduce the flying changes gradually, playfully, to take the drama out of a movement, which for some horses can be a significant source of stress during their education.

It was five years of endless research, considering all possible methods to help my gray stallion understand…of doubting…of wanting to give up…until the day when the "click" took place. I cannot say what triggered the sudden understanding in him. We were doing our "daily scales," switching from one exercise to another, looking once again for a way forward—and then something unbelievable happened. As if he suddenly had become weightless, he completed the movement, and in the same week we had not only the single flying changes, but also the four tempis, three tempis, and even two tempis. Each day, I tried the next level, without believing it would happen, and each time, Sultan amazed me by how easy it had suddenly become for him. A month and a half later, in Wels, Austria, he was doing the tempi changes in front of five thousand people, on the circle and with only the neck rope. It was unbelievable. It took me two more years to have them really straight and bigger, but they were there, and it was a huge victory.

The flying changes were a big step in our journey together, but there was another challenge the gray and I faced. As I mentioned earlier in these pages, after returning from the breeding center, Sultan became an extremely dominant stallion. For two and a half years I struggled to keep him and others safe, but in the barn he had become a true danger to himself.

It was finally with a very heavy heart that, at the end of spring 2014, I made the decision to have him castrated. It was a terrible moment. I felt like I was betraying him and couldn't even stay with him during the operation. I apologized a hundred times, crying in his box before leaving. But his self-inflicted injuries had been getting worse and worse, and I feared that one day an accident would be fatal. When his hormones took over, he had no survival instinct left. While his father was an extremely dominant stallion, as well, with regular outbursts of difficult behavior toward others, he nevertheless always took care of himself. His son, unfortunately, didn't.

My guilt became even worse when, after castration, serious complications appeared. My gray ran a 104-degree fever for more than a month, his wounds infected, without the vet available to help us. I had to attend to him myself every day, cleaning the surgical site, and watching him sink into feverish nothingness. We were in Belgium at that time, far from everybody we knew, and I was extremely lonely. It was already a very hard time in my life, and I thought now I had lost him forever. Even as his body was repaired, little by little, it seemed he had lost interest in life. Every morning, I turned him out in his pasture. Every day, a few hours later, I would find him exactly where I'd left him. He had not moved one foot. He had become totally disengaged from the world around him, and totally absent from himself.

He, who had once been so strong and brave, fearing absolutely nothing, now jumped at the slightest sound and was afraid of a ray of light on the ground. I didn't recognize my gray anymore. Seeing him in such a way broke my heart.

After trying to bring him back to life for several months, I finally decided, as a last resort, to send Sultan to my family in the South of France where our history together had begun, hoping he would regain some energy and a little zest for life. My parents cared for him while he rested in the field he grew up in, near the herd of retired ponies that had once driven him crazy. My family sent me pictures and videos of him every day, and little by little, I had the impression that he was slowly getting back to being himself. Mistral and I finally joined him a month later, happy to return to our roots after several months of very hard times.

During the fall of that same year, I went to Spain, accompanied by an acquaintance, to see some horses for an American friend, and because I was not sure Sultan would really ever fully come back. I didn't have the budget to buy a horse, but my friend had told me that in Andalusia there were very good three-year-olds for less than 5,000 euros (about 5,500 dollars), if I was willing to travel to the middle of nowhere. He convinced me to make a 48-hour trip and see for myself. That's how I met the one and only Raymond. A Corsican, the man with a mad energy and a golden heart, our guide who welcomed us into his house, took us everywhere in his four-wheel-drive (including the most unlikely places), and enabled me to meet someone who would change Sultan's destiny, and mine, forever.

I remember the moment: The stable was very dark. A very common-looking horse was led out of a stall. His back was too long, his hocks too weak, and he had a short neck that tied in poorly with his head. And yet, the man with him, Ismael Romero Arroyo, made the horse dance in complete freedom, right before our eyes. At the time, it seemed unreal that such a thing was possible, and I wanted to

understand how he did it, I wanted to find out how to do it myself, I wanted to learn. Since I only knew a few words of Spanish, I asked Raymond to ask Ismael if it was possible for me to come with my horse Sultan to work with him for a week. His immediate answer was no. He did not want "the French girl with flowers in her hair" at his home. And he was not teaching anymore, anyway, only taking in some horses from clients to teach them liberty tricks before sending them back. What he did was his own method, and he chose to pass it on only to a very close circle of acquaintances. I was sorely disappointed, and absolutely convinced that adding this man's knowledge to my classical dressage background was the next level I had to reach in my own education. Seeing my dismay, Raymond winked at me and told me to show Ismael videos of my work with Sultan and Mistral on my phone. I saw the man's curiosity piqued, and he finally grudgingly accepted Sultan and me as students.

Two weeks and over 900 miles later, Sultan and I were back in Sanlúcar de Barrameda. Mistral was also part of the trip, because we had been invited to participate in the Madrid 4* and would go there on our way back.

The arena was very small and sloping. There was no pasture. There were no paddocks, either. The three of us were forced out of our comfort zone during our stay, but it was worth it.

I wanted to take advantage of being there, so for the first two days, we tried a new approach to the piaffe with Mistral. But it did not give us a better result, so after that, he and I simply continued our usual daily routine together. We weren't there for him. For once, we were doing everything for his son...

Together, Sultan and I discovered groundwork, its principles, its rules, its basics, its foundation. Together, we took a new step toward freedom together. Of course, I already rode my white angel with the neck rope, as I did his father, but liberty on the ground was a whole new world. I also discovered the Spanish language, as it was not possible to use English with Ismael. It was one of the most interesting weeks of my life, where with the new knowledge and foreign language, my brain had to go faster, every single minute. Ismael became my friend. He taught me liberty work; I helped him with classical dressage. (We still help each other today, sharing our experiences and ideas to both continue to grow our understanding of horses.)

What he taught me that week was the primordial driver of comfort and discomfort that I had never really intellectualized until then. He also introduced the concept of leadership. As I have said in these pages, the horse is born with a gregarious instinct. He needs a leader to feel safe. If we don't behave as such, then the horse will have to assume that role. It's a matter of survival instinct. While I intuitively used these rules of the herd in a way, I didn't fully integrate them. Putting words to them allowed me to learn the concepts differently and employ them with awareness and purpose instead of instinct, over time. Too many people confuse everything these days, thinking they are being nice to their horses, when in fact they are ruining them by behaving the wrong way around them. I see it all the time

during clinics. Loving your horse means giving him straight lines and boundaries. For me, the main keys to horsemanship can be summarized in three words and in this order: *trust, respect, love*. Shared on both sides—horse and human. *That's* how you build a strong, powerful, deep relationship with a horse.

After our very intense work in Spain, we went home. It was time for Sultan and I to start our journey toward liberty, only the two of us, groping for the right answers. As on all paths we've traveled, we had some ups and downs, but it was the lows that made us grow, evolve, and understand the most important key lessons. Always.

Month after month, Sultan began to open up again, regaining his trust, his self-confidence, and his personality. His "sparkle" came back. My white angel made me discover the importance of managing energy. Today, I see my body during groundwork as a musical instrument, with tones and notes. It is an accordion I am playing all the time, every single second. Sultan made me understand how much I needed to learn to control my own body before attempting to help him control his. When we are riding, we can compensate for misplaced energy with our aids. But at liberty, there is no way out. Each wrong action, each wrong placement or posture, each misapplied emotion has an impact. You can't cheat. But when you finally reach a deep mastery of it, your body becomes the most interesting instrument to work with, and it translates to the saddle, as well. Only there can you truly reach another level of feel and understanding, full of nuance.

It's true I was lucky enough to be born with some instinct for being with horses, but that's not enough—far from it. It was necessary for me to learn to use my instincts correctly, to recognize my missteps and to analyze them in order to be able to overcome them. I had to learn to trust myself, as well, which was probably one of the most difficult steps for me. I had to learn to accept that I was allowed to make some mistakes, and I would surely make some, but that the worst thing I could do to Sultan was to doubt myself when I asked him to try an exercise, because a true mentor has answers to every question or situation; a true mentor wants to give confidence to those counting on him. If he wants to take them to the moon and back, he must first convince himself that it is possible. Doubting while asking something of a horse is betraying the trust of the one relying on you. Your horses will always forgive your mistakes, but they won't forgive you if you let them down. You need to overcome your own issues, fears, and emotions. That's why liberty work is so fascinating, and so important.

Having now made 90 percent of our groundwork discoveries working on our own, Sultan and I have, I believe, created a bit of our own rules, marked of course by the world from which I came—that of classical dressage. I am not ashamed to say that I have technical shortcomings in my liberty work, because what Sultan and I have built and achieved, and what I have done later on with others, thanks to him, we have done mostly out of instinct and trial-and-error. What we do on the ground is not based on established principles, such as those I can rely on in my classical dressage training. The truth is, I taught Sultan the movements I wished him to do at liberty mainly under the saddle, where I felt surer of my technique and knowledge, in order to help him feel them and understand them in his body so he could then be able to do it later on his own. It takes an incredibly smart horse to be able to do that...but that's who Sultan is—a horse with a very special intelligence and the ability to handle his body and his balance on his own, with just a few indications of my voice and the whip to help him place his shoulders and hips, and find the right rhythm.

When I train a horse for liberty, I always seek the same sensations as I would experience on his back. I can feel him as if I was on his back. I want him to be "in front of my inside leg" (which is, on the ground, represented by my body). That's the reason why I use a lot of micro-transitions, all the time, exactly the same way I do under saddle. It's one of my favorite basic exercises to use daily to help the horse move "from back to front," which is the way, in my eyes, to have the horse move in the most comfortable, fluid, balanced, and smooth way possible. The horse is a bit like an accordion, as well. If we learn to "play" with him correctly, the melody is sublime, filled with intense emotion and poetry. But if we play with him in the wrong way, the notes are discordant, hard, unpleasant. That's the image I always keep in mind while I am working with a horse.

As for the Spanish trot and canter, the very first steps Sultan took were not on purpose. For both, I was trying to help him to correct his balance with the whip at his inside shoulder, and in response, he offered a few incredible steps, which opened new possibilities in my mind. I hadn't ever seen a horse move in such a way before, so I couldn't search for them. They were my White Angel's gift.

To me, the basics of liberty work are exactly the same as those of classical dressage. It's all about balance, withers freedom, and hip placement. I look for my horses to bend around my body on the ground, exactly the same way they would bend around my inside leg if I was in the saddle. I try to make them always work from back to front, and not the other way around. All these details make the difference in the end, at least in the work I have achieved with Sultan over the years, and in what I have continued to build with other horses ever since. I don't pretend that my way is the right way. It is just the way I explore liberty. Sometimes, I wish I knew all the tricks so I could rely a bit more on recognized liberty methods rather than doing everything by trying, failing, thinking, learning, and doing it all again—til we find a way forward together. But that's not how liberty came into my life, and probably there is a reason for that. With time, Sultan gave me the basics of what has become "my way" of doing liberty. The liberty work I teach my students today is not mine, it's Sultan's.

My beautiful gray's journey has been more difficult than Mistral's, simply because he came after his illustrious father had built a following. Sultan didn't have a chance to start on small stages. He didn't have time to build himself quietly, in the shadows, where failure is noticed by fewer. His first performance was in March of 2016 in the huge stadium in Herning, Denmark, in front of 9,000 people who had high expectations after Mistral's show the year before. He didn't have the chance to take a bad step. From the moment he entered the spotlight, everyone—including me—expected him to behave just like his father at the peak of his career. It was a huge burden on Sultan's shoulders, a burden that became heavier when I discovered that my gray did not like being on stage at all. Instead of blossoming like Mistral did, becoming two times bigger when he entered the arena, Sultan sucked back, froze, lost half of his ability, and had his eye on the exit all the time. He didn't like it.

So, Sultan and I started a different journey together. As we were on tour, going from one show to another, in different countries, atmospheres, and environments, I started to take him for walks absolutely everywhere, several times per day, in any condition, with him free by my side. That was not easy at the beginning. I had to trust him first if I wanted him to trust me, too, but Sultan was a horse with very changeable emotions, which could lead sometimes to unexpected reactions or very grumpy moods. This was the reason why, a few months before our first performance, when I took Sultan again to Spain to meet another Spanish master from whom I wished to learn for a few days, I was told my gray would never, ever be a horse for liberty because he was much too "strong-minded" and "unreliable." My unicorn proved him wrong. Time and dedication were the answers. It wasn't easy, but it was worth it, and Sultan and I built the most important part of our relationship out of our long walks together, just the two of us, side by side.

For a long time, while each new movement was a source of excitement and curiosity for Sultan, as soon as it was learned and understood, he lost interest and started to look for problems that didn't exist. It was always the same pattern and has been a major source of anxiety for me, seeing as I did not rely on a proven method but worked by trial and error. I often had the feeling that I was "doing it wrong" and that everything was uncertain. Whenever this happened, I would doubt myself and think that all the work we had achieved together had been lost—until eventually I understood that this was just Sultan's way of processing things. Every time we fixed an exercise, another one was failing, and it just went on and on.

Then, about three years ago, this behavior disappeared entirely, probably because it no longer affected me in the same way. I knew my gray; I knew that whatever we had "lost" would come back the day after; I knew that it was all going to be okay…so the little "drama game" between us wasn't worth it anymore.

Sultan helped me gain confidence in our work and in who we are together. And without realizing it, this horse, who I had at first refused a place by my side, became my closest partner—even more so than his father. It is hard for me to write such a thing because Mistral will always remain my one and only, and my heart will always belong to him, but the trust I have in Sultan is beyond words. The struggles we went through during our journey and the fact neither of us gave up on the other brought us together in an unbreakable way. We are linked by the strongest bond. One we worked and fought for. He has become my second half, and I couldn't choose between the father and the son anymore.

Little by little, my gray has become my White Angel, albeit an angel who can have some very moody periods. The good news is that he never takes me by surprise. When he is having a bad day, you see it clearly on his face. He puts his "grumpy mask" on, and everybody is aware that Sultan is not available for the time being! During these episodes—which can last a few days, sometimes—every single thing, from cleaning his hooves to brushing his mane, from giving him a meal to working on an exercise, is a cause for grumbling. But here again, I now know that it's okay, that it's just who he is, and we—my team and I—have to accept his moods and let him be. The best answer I have found is to basically ignore it, just go easy for a couple of days and play outside, only doing things he usually likes, until he is back in a happier place. I used to try to "bring him to his senses" and asked him to deal with his emotions. That was a mistake. Once I started leaving him to his moods when they showed up,

respecting them without letting them "take up too much space," they no longer came between us. I can now even see sometimes that he makes an effort on his own to overcome his bad temper—acknowledging it on his own, now that I don't ask him to do it anymore. It took all the time we spent together and the trials we went through together for us to reach the level of understanding, inner peace, and mutual unfailing trust we now enjoy. We know each other by heart. Like an old married couple, I learned to love his flaws, weaknesses, and vulnerabilities, and I think I can say that he learned to love mine too. This is what makes our partnership indestructible today.

As I wrote earlier, during the summer of 2018, Sultan experienced a major colic episode, which necessitated a trip to the veterinary clinic. There he contracted a bacterium that attacked his entire nervous system. (It is impossible for me now to remember the name of the bacterium—my brain has erased it.) He couldn't stand. He'd fall against the walls, he'd fall to the ground, and he couldn't get up. The vet told me Sultan might not survive, and if he did survive, the long-lasting effects from his illness could be severe. This didn't matter to me. I couldn't let him go. I wanted to save him, no matter what.

Sultan fought, and he won. His recovery took months, but even more incredible, not only did he become himself again, but he continued to grow in

With Louise, in my belly and then
in the saddle, and Sultan.

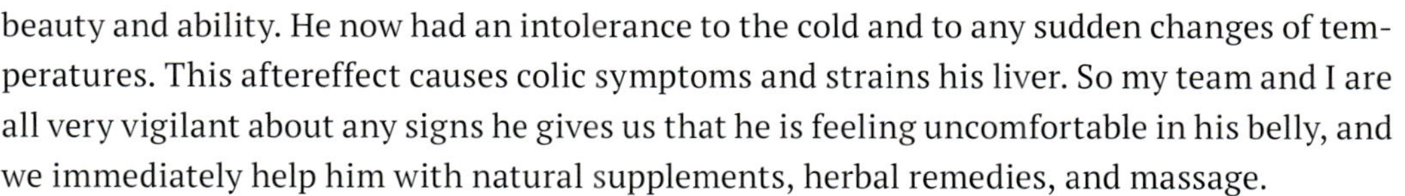

beauty and ability. He now had an intolerance to the cold and to any sudden changes of temperatures. This aftereffect causes colic symptoms and strains his liver. So my team and I are all very vigilant about any signs he gives us that he is feeling uncomfortable in his belly, and we immediately help him with natural supplements, herbal remedies, and massage.

For a number of years, but even more recently, and especially because of Sultan, I have adapted my training work to adjust according to the information related to the horses' physical and mental well-being that my team gives me every single day, before and after each practice time. We all work very closely with our horses as I believe that this is the only way to know and understand them as completely as possible. This helps me avoid doing exercises that may not fit on a certain day due to soreness or other concerns, but which won't be a problem at all the day after, with the appropriate support given to the horse in between.

It is thanks to Sultan that my research for improving the welfare of my horses has gone in new directions. It is because of him that I have started to examine and better understand the composition of their diet compared to their needs, and that I have learned the properties of herbs, essential oils, Bach flowers, and other natural remedies. My team and I then learned how to use them in the most efficient way, taking into account each horse's physical and mental characteristics, as well as their ongoing growth and development. I have met fascinating and incredible people, all of whom pursue the same goal as I do: better understanding of our horses in order to give them better lives and care for them in the most natural way. I have always taken into account the well-being of my horse companions and been interested in natural

medicine, but recently, it has become an obsession—a duty. I am always trying products, developing others, or creating new ones. And it started with him. It started *for* him. Sultan made me look at the bigger picture.

During this time, my golden-haired princess, my Louise, was born, and unlike Mistral, who was jealous of her, Sultan immediately took care of her with infinite precaution. As for Louise, as soon as she was old enough to hold his rope in her tiny hands while he was grazing, she couldn't let him go. Her heart chose him among all the others. Watching them grow together has completed the puzzle. Sultan belongs to her even more than to me. The love and trust my daughter and my White Angel share is something I've never seen before between such a big horse and a very young lady. She can ask him anything, and he will always try his heart out for her, while taking care to keep her safe. Together, they are my sunshine. Every time I see them with one another, my heart melts.

I still had one regret left: not having been able to show the true Sultan to the world—the one *I* know…the very special one. Under the spotlights, on a stage, even though he had made great progress, he had never been able to show his true self—he always hung back, always became smaller. I felt I hadn't yet done justice to who he had become, because in his own way, Sultan had become as extraordinary as his father.

Earlier in these pages I wrote about March of 2022, when we were all together—father and son, mother and daughter—at

Equitana for the show of a lifetime in Essen, Germany. However, Sultan had not performed in public for two years, and I knew that this time, with a four-year-old girl on his back, having him "shut down in his world" was not an option. So we prepared for the performance in a way we never had before, aiming to have him feel perfectly safe in all circumstances. I created a detailed training plan, beginning a month before, to prepare him for the challenges I knew he would face in front of a crowd, but also leaving him time to find his comfort zone within himself, as well, especially during the sound of applause, which he had never liked.

Everything was going perfectly, so my team and I were super relaxed and confident, when life decided to put a spoke in the wheel. Ten days before the show, a series of unfortunate events,

all beyond my control, upended all our plans. I then only had one goal in mind: building a "safety bubble" around Sultan so that negative emotions couldn't reach him and overwhelm him.

And somehow, we made it.

During the first rehearsal in the Hop Top Show arena in Essen, I started by working with Sultan to help him deal with his emotions during the sound of applause. It was very important to transfer his acceptance to the new environment. I could see the stress in his eyes at first, but he calmed down quickly and his body started to relax. Then, we performed the show once through without Louise. Although he performed the movements without technical mistakes, I could see him starting to "suck back" and retreat "inside." That's when something quite magical happened: As soon as I put Louise on his back, Sultan's attitude completely

changed. He took over his emotions. My team and I could clearly see that taking care of her was more important to him than anything else around.

That was the exact moment I knew I could count on him from now on. And, night after night, show after show, I watched him "grow up" in the spotlights, gaining more and more confidence, opening up, and enjoying performing—finally.

For the first time, I was able to relax by his side on the stage and enjoy dancing with him as if we were at home. He was there, fully present, grounded, serene, peaceful. It was one of the greatest moments of my life. One of the most rewarding, as well. One of the few very precious memories that I will cherish my entire life and that nothing will ever be able to erase or tarnish. Our circle had been completed—together, the four of us.

If I were asked to use only one word to describe my feelings for Sultan, *grateful* is the one I would use.

"

Thank you, Sultan, for everything you taught me. Thank you for everything you gave me. Thank you for all you have helped me understand. Thank you for all you have helped me discover. Thank you for our failures and misunderstandings. Thank you for every second of this dented and imperfect journey that has allowed me to grow so much as a horsewoman as well as a person. Thank you for never giving up, my Sultan. Thank you. For simply being you, that extraordinary horse who looks like no other, especially not your father, and who I have learned, year after year, to love with all my heart.

Our little golden gangster, Pirate.

Pirate

The smallest one who still somehow took up the most space

Pirate was just over 9 hands high, but had the personality of a giant. This amazing little golden pony entered my life like a surprise tornado. I was in Spain at the request of a friend from the United States who wanted me to try some horses for him. Around the corner of a small barn, I saw the tip of a curious little nose, reaching over the stall door to see what was happening. It seemed clear he did not get out of that little stall very often, but he had that special sparkle in his eyes. That very shiny *something*. My heart accelerated when I opened his door and discovered him entirely. His owner told me he couldn't keep him—he needed to sell the pony quickly because he needed money and had no time for him. I had absolutely no idea what I was going to do with this character, but I knew immediately he was a new member of our family.

Working with Pirate at liberty was a new challenge for me, as I had to find a different way to communicate what I wanted than the method I used with Sultan.

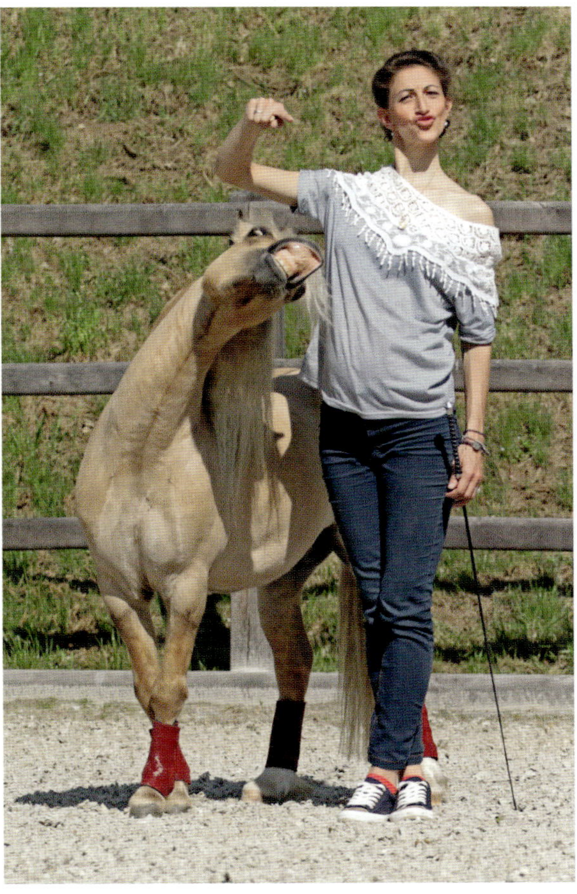

I came home, got my truck, and drove back to Spain again in nine hours. My family disapproved that I had agreed to take this little Welsh with a gorgeous head but a temper on fire. They weren't wrong. The golden pony was only four years old, and I didn't know what I was going to do with him. I had absolutely no plan. I just followed my heart. Taking him home was the obvious choice to me.

In the end, it did not take Pirate much time to win everyone's love. He was the most endearing, charismatic, sweet, and hilarious of all our four-legged gangsters. If the character of Jack Sparrow (*Pirates of the Caribbean*) were reincarnated as a pony, he would have been this golden troublemaker named Pirate.

While he already knew some groundwork and tricks, he had never experienced it at liberty. He had been trained to play the part of a "bull" in a show (which he actually never performed), chasing a broom masquerading as a bullfighter's cape. It left him with the bad habit of biting. I managed to quell the reflexive behavior at home, but it came out again, as soon as he found himself outside his comfort zone, facing stress during performances.

Pirate was a free and wild soul who took up all the space, wherever he went. If he had been born a human, he would certainly have been a stand-up comic, performing one-man shows with crazy success. He's the only pony or horse I've ever known with such a natural sense of humor. It wasn't because I asked him to do some funny things. No, Pirate didn't need me to be hilarious. It was just who he was—an innate clown, who truly enjoyed making people laugh. Did he ever really listen to me? The honest answer is no—not as my other horses did. In the way of a spoiled child, he did what he wanted, whenever he wanted. I was very well aware of it. But it was okay with me, and because it was okay, with time, he gave me some trust. In the end, when it was just the two of us, we played together like the best friends in the world, and that's truly who we were. We managed to put in place our

own rules where each of us respected the other and gave the other space. He was free to do his own things, and because he was, he stayed with me. He had a generosity that was matched only by his intelligence, and he had incredible expressions that made him irresistible. It was terribly difficult to ever stay serious with him during training.

Pirate was a new challenge for me because, as I explained, with Sultan, I produced our liberty work by matching vocal cues to what I taught him under the saddle. With this tiny pony, I had to find new keys to the training, as obviously I couldn't ride him. It made me explore different avenues of reflection and research. He also opened my eyes to the fact that, even when only as high as three apples on one knee, a pony can have as much ability as any horse, if we work him with the same quality and the same attention. To accompany our liberty training, my golden pony had a stretching routine on the longe line to strengthen his topline and one for proprioception to help him develop and improve his balance. I created a real program to make him feel good, comfortable, and strong in his body. I did discover, however, that I could never do the longeing myself because, too accustomed to the liberty work and "playtime" he had with me, he would try to present everything I had taught him (rather than doing the longeing circle like he was supposed to), and he would not understand why I would tell him that he was wrong when he was putting his heart into proudly displaying all his tricks. To avoid any misunderstanding, I made the decision to leave the longeing work to others so that it remained clear to him that these workouts were different than our liberty time. This system worked perfectly, although there was not a single person on whom he didn't play small jokes during the first few longe circles, always testing a little.

Pirate was this gangster pony who, when turned out in the pasture, spent lots of time scratching himself on Sultan, like the big gray was a tree, just because Pirate knew how much he annoyed

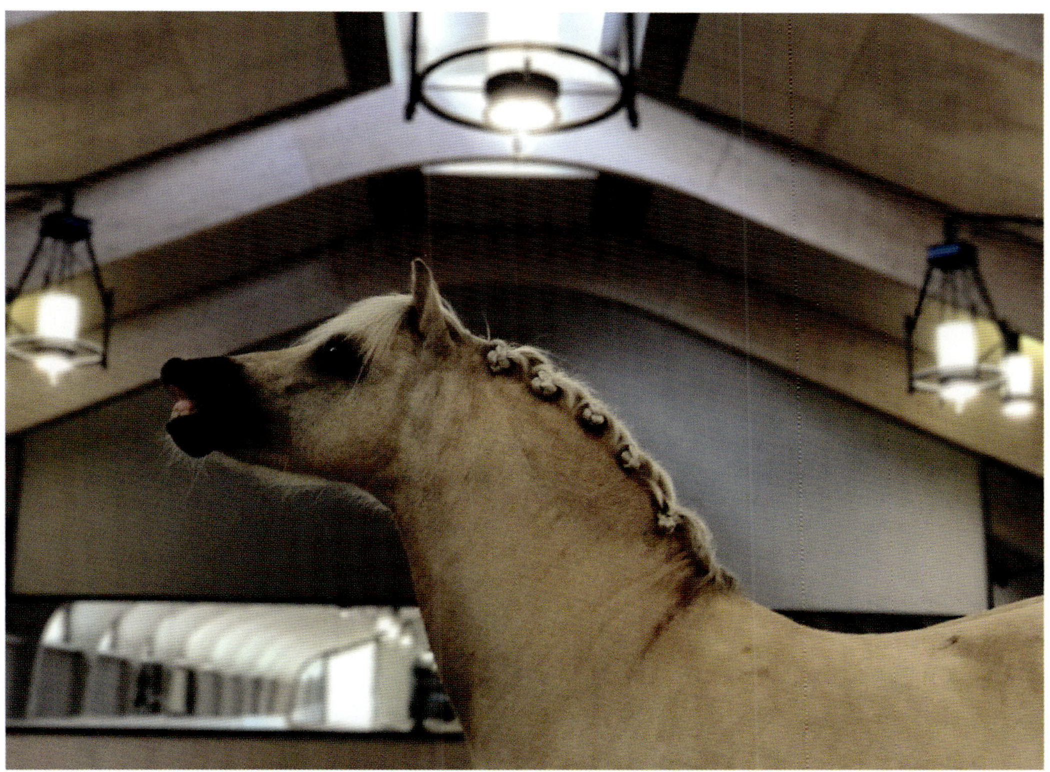

Sultan by doing that. He was this pony who stopped everyone in his path, because he was so handsome. He was this pony who, with his clownish expressions, always had a crowd of people standing in front of his stall wherever we were, in awe of his special soul.

Pirate demanded everybody's attention, all the time. And he got it—from everyone. In the same way he had taken my heart in Spain, he had this habit of pushing his little nose over the door as soon as he heard some noise nearby, and, having learned to "smile" by curling his upper lip up since then, he began to do it at everyone passing by in order to get a hug or a carrot.

At home he had become the most incredible liberty pony, but I could never show who he really was in a performance. It wasn't his destiny. It wasn't his story. During the fall of 2015, when I had him along for his first tour by the side of my black and white heroes to discover Europe and what it was like on stage, a bad experience closed the doors of this world to us, for good.

Watching my pony work with me backstage early one morning, the organizers of the show I was doing with Mistral asked me if I could host the prize-giving ceremony with Pirate. He was about to be five years old, and while he was still very young, I thought it could be a good and easy start for him in front of a crowd. It was a big mistake that I would long regret.

After Pirate proudly brought the awards to the winners and made the whole stadium laugh with his tomfoolery, the event organizers forgot to let us exit the arena before launching the lap of honor. Faced with sudden and very loud music, a cheering crowd, stamping their feet in the stands, and the winning horses, galloping full speed around the ring, a complete panic seized Pirate. He hadn't been prepared for such an event. I had a hard time getting him out of the arena. The stress caused him to sweat so profusely he was covered with white foam

With Pirate and Louise.

within a minute, and he bit me quite hard on my belly. His eyes were rolled back in fear. He couldn't control himself.

After that unfortunate episode, I continued to take Pirate with us on the road. He was part of the family. We could peacefully practice his liberty work backstage, gaining new experience in many kinds of environments—discovering the sea in Malmö, Sweden, and in Germany, playing in the parks of Hamburg and enjoying the grass of Aachen. It was inconceivable for me not to have him by our sides during our adventures. But while we were able to perform some masterclasses to small audiences in Germany and Sweden, explaining and showing our work together, the few times Pirate was again in real "show" conditions, with lights or an audience too close to him, it turned into a disaster. His only concern in those situations was to escape as soon as possible. So, after an attempt in Hannover in December 2017, which was my last try after having given him a complete year off, I made the decision never to ask him to perform in front of an audience again.

We must accept that some horses and ponies are destined for a different path than the one we have in mind for them. If you want to let them shine, and become the best version of themselves, your job is to listen to what they tell you.

In the meantime, Louise was born. She was four days old when I put her on the back of my little golden pony for the first time. She fell asleep there, peacefully, and he, usually impossible to hold in place for more than 30 seconds, had remained still and calm.

At that special moment, Pirate's unexpected arrival in my life two years earlier suddenly made sense. We knew each other by heart, he was my everyday sunshine, and he was going to become my daughter's best friend. Together, we took long walks in the park, the three of us. And what was Louise's favorite thing to do? To hold his reins in her tiny hands while he was grazing. I could watch them together for hours.

With her, "Pirate the Gangster" transformed day after day into "Piratou," a very sweet pony who took wonderful care of his little girl. With us adults, he still remained this huge and shiny personality, but as soon as Louise was there, he was different. It took a little while for the transformation to complete. The big change happened when Louise and I arrived and settled in Belgium. Every time he heard her voice, his little ears stood up. He watched her from his meadow. He took her under his wing.

By the time she was two, Louise was having fun asking Pirate to do the Spanish walk, to lie down, or to smile, and as a model student, he hurried to do everything she asked him with a generosity and a focus that still make me smile when I think back to those days. He gave her a taste for the liberty work. He taught her how to use her body and energy naturally. He was the most thoughtful schoolmaster. Who would have thought that this clown with a fiery temperament would be transformed by the side of a little girl? I think I can say that he welcomed her truly into his heart, in a different way than he had with me years before. He took care of her. He looked after her. He seemed suddenly responsible. He was no longer the little troublemaker. Another soul had taken the place of the "baby of the family."

But in the spring of 2020, on a cursed day of May, the exact date of which my heart has erased, Pirate was taken away from us, opening in me a gaping hole. I remember seeing him from the window of my kitchen while I was eating dinner with Louise, lying in an unusual way in his field. An alarm went off in my head, and I immediately called Ornella, a member of my team, who went to get him up. At

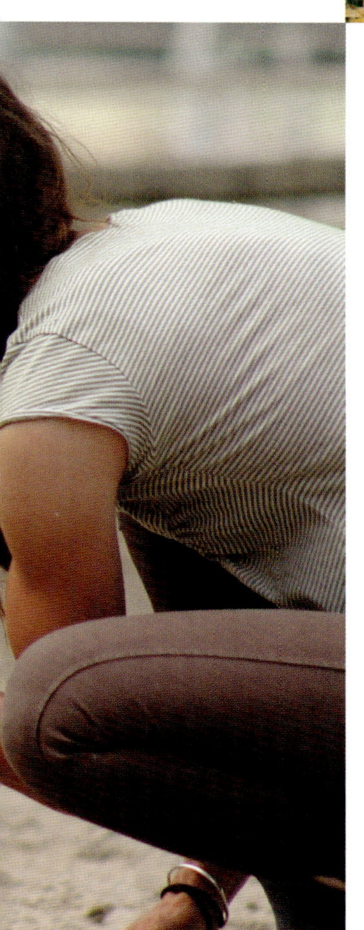

ten in the evening, our veterinarian advised us to take him to the clinic because he was not experiencing a "normal" colic.

The next day, Pirate seemed to be recovering, and the vet told me on the morning of the second day that I could come and pick him up. I was at a meeting at the bank when my phone rang—the clinic was calling again. Pirate's condition had suddenly crashed. I was told to come immediately as he might not have long to live.

I left everything at the bank, jumped in the car, and raced to the clinic, where I was about to live out one of the most traumatic moments of my life.

When I arrived, panicked, my golden pony was unrecognizable, covered in sweat, unable to stand, refusing to eat. I was desperate. After an hour of massaging him, holding him in my arms, supporting him, reassuring him, a glimmer of hope came. The vet told me that since my arrival, Pirate's vital signs were settling and his general state was improving. So I continued what I was doing, trying to give him my energy, begging him not to leave us. He even managed to eat a bit from my hands.

But suddenly, Pirate's condition worsened again. The result of blood samples taken two hours apart was a grim verdict. Refusing to believe it, I asked the veterinarian why he had improved at all if he had always been condemned. She replied that he had given me the last of what he had to give, but that if I did not let him go now, he would experience great suffering, before an inevitable end that was now only a matter of hours away.

So I asked him to lie down for the last time, took his head in my arms, and stayed with him as he drew his last breath. Eventually letting go is part of our lives when we live with horses, and it is always very painful. But this time was devastating. My breath went away from me with his last sigh. That life that dies out… that beloved soul that abandons a body, now empty.

It took me more than an hour to be able to breathe properly again. The pain was so insane that it overturned everything in its path. I couldn't speak. I couldn't think. I had gone into a world of shadows. For the second time in my life, a part of me had passed away forever, and the indescribable agony came at a time when my life had shifted just a few months before into chaos and a profound sorrow. Already down on one knee, already facing the most hurtful failure I'd yet had to go through in my personal life, something in

me broke deeply the day I lost Pirate. It was as if the dam that I had been desperately holding in place for months had cracked under this new ordeal, flooding and overwhelming everything in its way.

After the sadness, the emptiness, the absolute refusal to accept the reality of what had taken place, I had to face an unusual feeling for me. Anger. Anger in the face of injustice. Anger in the face of this immense loss for my daughter and for me. Anger at those who remained while he was gone. A devastating, consuming anger that I tried to smother but that devoured me from the inside.

I thought I'd been changed forever. I thought I would never again be the person I was before. I thought I had lost my faith in life. But while it is true today I do remain severed from a part of myself, the loss of our golden pony allowed me to reach a new level of understanding, to question myself deeply again, to go further in

my journey, leading me to become a new version of myself—much stronger, much more centered, much more grounded. If I have lost my naivety, my lightness, and the carefree sensibility of my childhood, I have gained a better understanding of others, empathy, and compassion. My view of the world and the people around me has changed. I added many shades to my perceptions.

Life has showed me that you can't predict your future, as the challenges you will meet along the way will turn you into someone different, with new expectations, needs, and priorities. While I continue to discover, day after day, where I *want* to go and what I'd like to be the next step, I also now know, very clearly, what I *don't* want to experience, be, or accept anymore. That has probably been the hardest "new skin" to enter, and I've done so with a lot of struggle and sorrow, but in the end, an inner peace has come with each terrible pain. I am indeed not the same anymore... and I never will be. My little amazing golden pony made me rise from the ashes with new eyes.

Louise was so small when Pirate joined Peter Pan in Wonderland...but she didn't forget him. Ever. It took me a long time to be able to explain to her that he would never come back without falling apart. With the arrival of other ponies in her life, I thought that gradually her memory would erase our special little golden boy. But since his departure, not a day has gone by that she has not talked about him. She sees him all over—as much as I do. In our yard, where she remembers him walking his last steps at home. In the clouds, when she finds a funny shape. In the stars, on beautiful nights. Pirate is gone, but he is still everywhere, and as long as we are breathing, he will continue to live within us.

Hermès' beauty is unparalleled. He is like a painter's masterpiece come to life.

Hermès

The talented colossus who needed me to think for him

I would have liked to have written in these pages about Ballerina, Naxos, Aslan, and Walkuere, who left, each of them, an indelible print on my heart, even if our paths only crossed for a short while. I would have liked to tell you about Sir Rubinstein, Di Magic, and Ehrendof, who enabled me to experience emotional moments in the competitive international dressage arena. Not telling their story here—*our* story— makes me feel guilty, as if I am not honoring their place in my life and my journey as I should. But I have to make choices, and the one I've made for this book is, perhaps surprisingly, to tell you of a horse that I could never truly feel close to or attached to, despite his undeniable talent and numerous qualities.

Maybe telling our story here is a way to make amends for never being able to let him enter my heart. Maybe this is a way to finally let him take a place by my side, as in his own way, he played an important role in my journey.

If there is one thing I am sure of, it is that we cross paths along life's way with the horses who will make us grow, one way or another, at the moment we have to. There is no coincidence. Each horse has a reason to be by your side when the right time comes.

Hermès came into my life to take over from Mistral. It was an impossible task to accomplish, for any horse. That, I came to understand with time, thanks to him. I had perhaps already made a similar mistake with Sultan years before, but with Hermès, life made the challenge different. Now I know that I will never aim for such a thing again. My lesson is learned, and it has been an important revelation, which has led me to rethink and see my future through another lens, with a quiet heart.

This white colossus with a black mane, tail, and legs is a monument toward which everybody turns, even those generally unmoved by Lusitanos. He is magnificent, impressive, powerful. He could be one of Géricault's famous paintings come alive or the reincarnation of Alexander the Great's Bucephalus. Each of his curves, each of his lines, is perfect. At work, he is supple as a cat and strong as a bull.

But while his body can do anything, his head can't. It took me a long time to figure this out, and even longer to accept it.

Hermès came to me from Portugal at six years old. He had a very restless and difficult mouth, making the contact complicated and very unstable, causing him not to be able to use his back properly. I tried everything—with many kinds of bits...without...with many kinds of nosebands...without. Nothing really worked, until by searching myself and all that I was doing every single day with him, asking myself questions about every aspect of his riding and his care, I found the two answers that would change everything.

The first thing I figured out, was that, having extremely huge shoulders, Hermès felt "trapped" in any dressage saddle, and this feeling led him to defensive reactions whenever I asked him for movements where his shoulder freedom was at stake. The day I decided to ride him only with a bareback pad and to remove the saddle from his daily life, a big weight seemed to lift. He never got angry again. He continued to have trouble understanding what I was expecting from him sometimes, but in a completely different way. Instead of getting annoyed and resentful, he tried very hard to find a way to successfully do what I was asking. Instead of going against me without even giving it a shot, he was finally willing to give all he had.

While I had known for a while that saddle fit was a problem for him, I lost way too much time trying a lot of other things before doing what I should have done from day one. I blamed myself mercilessly for that. I should have tried the bareback pad sooner. *Of course! How stupid of me.* The thing was, I had thought my relationship with Hermès wasn't strong enough for me to ride him bareback, when in fact, our relationship was stuck in large part because of the saddle issue. I didn't follow my inner voice as I should have, when she had been giving me the answer for several months already. (Today, I ride absolutely all my horses bareback, some during each training session, others only from time to time because they need to remain used to the saddle, but all of them feel freer in their movement without the wooden piece that is the saddle tree on their back. Of course, this works only if we, as riders, have a balanced and quiet seat; otherwise, we would damage the horse's spine.)

The second answer I found with Hermès was a deeper lesson learned. Ever since I was a kid, I've had a lot of trouble dealing with stupidity. I truly struggle to understand it, which leads me to struggle even more to have empathy for it. Yet, some are born less smart and less quick than others. That's just life.

I guess during my "adulthood" of riding horses before Hermès, I had always crossed paths with clever horses. Although many of them were far from my giant's equal in natural physical ability, and all of course had very different personalities, temperaments, and histories, they were all bright. This innate intelligence enabled me to lead them toward the empowerment and self-reliance that are so important to me in the path I have chosen to take, and later on, to build, year after year, with each of the horses who have shared a piece of my journey.

Autonomy and independence. Empowerment. My obsession. My way of freeing horses from us at the end of their "apprenticeship" under us, when they are all grown up. Giving them a voice. I teach them everything with this final Holy Grail goal of leading them to a grounded independence where we respect and trust each other enough to reach *freedom*. And by freedom, I don't mean riding with just the neck rope or doing liberty tricks. I mean, knowing your horse by heart, his strengths and weaknesses, in order to push him every single day, like you would do with your own child, to grow, flourish, and become the best version of himself, for himself—while leaving him the choice of what and who he will ultimately become.

It is Hermès who has helped me put some words to and intellectualize that "autonomy" part. I had long talked about trust, respect, and mentorship, which are, for me, the absolute fundamental keys in a horse's education, development, and happiness, but for a long time I couldn't tell you toward what exactly I am constantly pushing them. Now I can clearly say that, even if it makes working with a horse sometimes more complicated (big personalities often require a lot more time and many more "discussions" this way), I want my horses to think, participate, and be responsible for themselves. I want them to be *part of it*—of everything we do—not to be there only because they have no choice.

Hermès has been, for a long time, my failure. The one who made all my beliefs fall apart. Until him, this idea of an "earned freedom" had succeeded with all my horses. I watched them bloom and gain confidence—all of them, except him. The more I forced him to "empower himself," the more I pushed him to think by himself, the more he was lost and panicked. I then thought that I no longer knew how to ride a horse in the way I wanted to. That I had lost my feel, my understanding. I questioned everything with him—myself first. Because even if I said out loud many times that Hermès had crazy talent but a slower comprehension, another part of me refused to accept this idea. I couldn't grasp that I was just on the wrong track with him. That my beliefs about where his happiness *should* lie were just inaccurate. I was so convinced by what I had discovered by the side of all the horses before him that I forgot how much each of them is different, and that for some horses, including my handsome colossus, the responsibility of autonomy is too heavy to bear.

As soon as I accepted that empowerment was not Hermès' answer, that he needed help, guidance, and support to feel safe, our entire relationship changed, and a new world opened its doors for us. His own fulfillment wasn't where *I* wanted to see it. His safe and happy place was when I was thinking for him, and before him.

During our journey, before I found my two answers, I had tried twice to ride him with the neck rope, which turned out to be hopeless since, desperate to have something to hold onto, to have someone compensate for his balance and body, he turned on himself like a fish

With Hermès, giving him independence was not the answer. He needed me to support him.

in his bowl. What is surprising in our story is that when I finally accepted that freedom was not his answer, we managed to reach this milestone a few months later.

I will forever remember that day where everything became suddenly so clear and limpid to me, when a huge weight lifted from my shoulders. That morning, I woke up knowing that we were going to try it again. My gorgeous gray was constantly progressing, and far more serene since I had begun helping him and supporting him much more, instead of always trying to push him to understand, and from this serenity, a new confidence was starting to grow in him—which, ironically, led him to a little independence. I expected nothing more from the session than to be able to walk, trot, and possibly canter on the track. This, for me, would already be a huge win. But that day Hermès showed me just how much he had grown up, how much he had changed, how much he had transformed over the past few months. After some timid first steps, I saw him understand what he was finally capable of, and the movements then just chained together: a few strides of piaffe, a bit of collected trot, a pirouette in each direction, and at the end, the two tempis. I couldn't believe it myself.

The answer was not only accepting who he was, but also letting go of others' expectations. Because yes, once Mistral had become a star recognized around the world, I had to learn to live with the weight of people's expectations, every single day. I was no longer anonymous, but had to answer questions, show, demonstrate, prove, explain, even defend myself some-times from individuals I had never even met but who were absolutely certain they knew everything about me and my work. And then there was social media and the virtual world, where destroying those out there *trying* was a daily activity for some damaging—and probably damaged—persons. I know that some of them are not even aware of what they do, and how much what they write comes from their own failures, frustrations, bitterness, sadness, and also, sometimes, misunderstandings, lack of knowledge, or even deeply held beliefs. We can

claim that it does not matter to us, that it does not affect us, that
it does not change us, and maybe for some lucky ones, it doesn't.
But for me, as someone who always doubted myself, it has been
hard to be able to cope with these kinds of injustices. It gave me
a hard outside shell for years, and although I was very well aware
of it, I hadn't measured its power and impact on my daily life. I felt
I had to justify my life and what I did with it. I felt I had to rebuild
a new Mistral and a new Sultan to deserve and earn it.

I've never been more wrong.

There is a quote I am very fond of: "Those who think it is
impossible, please do not disturb those who are trying." I would
add to it: "by inventing things and stories that never happened
only to justify your incomprehension when the impossible becomes
possible."

*In the end, our only judges are the horses by our side.
The rest is nothing but wind.*

I truly believe that the day when, rather than judging
systematically, humans instead try to understand each other
and to work hand in hand, the world will be a much better place
to live, for us as well as our animals. It will allow us all to grow
in unexpected ways, our lives enhanced by others' experiences,
journeys, stories, and research.

Today, thanks to Hermès, and rich from all my own past
experiences, I feel freed from the societal expectations and
pressure I felt before, and this is one of the biggest gifts a horse
has given to me. There will be no second Mistral. There will be no
second Sultan either. Every story is different. For years, those two
horses were my whole world. Today, a little girl with blond curls
has taken that spot. I will never ever be the same again. I have new
dreams, new hopes. It doesn't change my love, my passion, and
my admiration for these magnificent animals. On the contrary,
I just now want and need to share other things with them.
It is a new turn in my evolution, and there are no words big enough
to express how grateful I am to have had the chance to meet
each one of these extraordinary souls and share with them this
incredibly rich journey.

With Hermès.

DENOUEMENT

Life always has you cross paths
with the horse from whom you have
something to learn at a specific time
in your personal journey.
I am one hundred percent
convinced of this today.

With Mistral, my heart.

This does not necessarily mean that every horse will take an important place in your heart. As with other humans, we are not made to get along with all horses, and that's okay. Some impact us forever; others come to teach us something we have to understand before simply continuing on their way. It took me a long time to figure this out and to be able to accept it without feeling guilty, because on the other hand, as Antoine de Saint Exupéry said, "You are forever responsible for what you have tamed."

I used to say that Mistral and Sultan came way too early in my life because building other stories after such two very special ones is nearly an impossible goal to achieve. But I was wrong. They were there right on time, before I became a mother. Before my entire world changed as well as my priorities. Lately, I have felt the need more and more to share and explore different things with the horses by my side. The time has come to take a new road. I have no idea yet of which one it will be exactly. The only thing I know is the horses will show me the way, as each of them has always done.

There is one thought that has particularly stuck with me during the past few years, in this new society where everything has to go faster and faster. I have been struggling with the speed of things, as well, trying to "keep up," so I know it is an important clue to the next stage of my journey:

TIME *is the only answer.* You can't avoid it. You can't replace it. You can't buy it. All the technique in the world can never ever replace TIME when you want to build a true special bond with your horse.

TIME
is the only answer.

With Mistral.

ACKNOWLEDGMENTS

Many thanks...

To my little angel, my everything, my wonderful Louly, for giving me some strength every day. You have been my power to tell each of these stories. I hope from the bottom of my heart that the day you will be old enough to read it, you will like this book, because I wrote it for you, above all.

To the ponies and horses with whom I have shared moments of life. I apologize to all those I have not spoken about in these pages. You have each brought and taught me so much. A special mention for Ballerina and Walkuere who have been two very special souls in my life. A part of me stayed with each of you.

To my mom who first passed along to me this consuming passion, then taught me to love horses for what they are and not for what they give us. To you who showed me the infinite paths to follow and who always believed in me, whatever my choices have been. Thank you for allowing me to follow my dreams. Teaching me that magic does really exist when you choose to see it. Pushing me to seek the beauty everywhere.

To my brother Morgan, with whom I had the chance to share so many moments of life, forever engraved. My heart holds fast to the image of this little boy, sitting on the feeder in the horse stall, giving me the thread and the needle while I braided Germanicus's mane, making riddles to pass the time. That was in Saumur. You were 11. I was 21. We covered almost 1,000 miles in four days, me with an open cut on my finger, which you helped me bandage each day. We did the Grand Prix U25 international competition, only the two of us, without a coach, without a groom, without help. People looked at us curiously when we passed by, me on Germanicus, you by my side, happily holding a grooming bucket, camera around your neck. That weekend you would take what would become one of the emblematic photos of the Haras National du Pin. When we were together, nothing felt scary anymore, and this is one of the most powerful strengths one can feel.

To my adoptive father Jean-Marc. Ponies and horses often took a lot of space in our life, but you always made sure to help and made things possible, even when they were complicated. I know it hasn't always been easy for you to understand my choices, but in the end, you see, they got me to become what you always said I was born to be: a writer.

To Sauveur and Catherine Vaisse for having bred the two horses of my life, Mistral and Sultan du Coussoul, and for having trusted me during all these years.

To my friends for sharing the laughter and the tears, the joy and the pain. Thank you for being there, even in silence, sometimes.

I am forever grateful.

To all those who have accompanied and supported us, my horses and me, for a few days or a few years. I do not forget you. You are part of our history.

To Mathieu, for your review full of kindness, well hidden behind your scathing humor. I am still laughing while thinking of it, and it feels good.

To Hubert Perring, for teaching me so much during these 15 years and for always believing in us—Mistral and me. Without you the path would have been different.

To Laurent Faucheur, Marcel Delestre, Mustapha El Bahjaoui, Didier Cazalet, Fabien Godelle, Philippe Limousin, and Alain Francqueville. Each of you, in your own way, at different moments in my life, has been the centerpiece of the puzzle of my destiny.

To all the show organizers who have trusted us across Europe, and sometimes a little farther, especially Sophie and Tina from Equitana, the team from the Sweden International Horse Show, that from Aachen, Fabien Galle from Les Crinières d'Or, and the very special team from Roma's Piazza del Poppolo, which has provided what will always remain incredible memories to me. Thank you all for giving us so many opportunities and allowing us to live a dream.

To Zoé, Andréa, and Laurine, who allowed me, through the trust I have in them, to free up time to go through the last corrections of this book. You are my forever "Dream Team."

To my editor, Rebecca Didier, and Trafalgar Square Books Managing Director Martha Cook, for your support, kindness, and trust. I hope this book is up to your expectations. I wrote it with my heart.

Finally, many thanks to you, dear readers, for taking the time to travel with me. This book was not easy to write. It is a part of me, but it is above all a part of the horses who made me that I entrust to you, and I am happy to know that as long as your memories and your hearts will keep them warm, they will continue to live through you.

Alizée Froment

– WITH PIRATE –